Leadership
through the Ages

Ronald D. Sylvia
San Jose State University

WAVELAND

PRESS, INC.

Long Grove, Illinois

For information about this book, contact:
Waveland Press, Inc.
4180 IL Route 83, Suite 101
Long Grove, IL 60047-9580
(847) 634-0081
info@waveland.com
www.waveland.com

10-digit ISBN 1-57766-621-6
13-digit ISBN 978-1-57766-621-9

Printed in the United States of America

7 6 5 4 3 2 1

Leadership
through the Ages

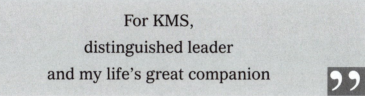

For KMS,
distinguished leader
and my life's great companion

Contents

Introduction

> And it came to pass on the morrow, that Moses sat to judge the people: and the people stood by Moses from the morning unto the evening.
>
> And when Moses' father-in-law saw all that he did to the people, he said, What is this thing that thou doest to the people? Why sittest though thyself alone, and all the people stand by thee from morning unto even?
>
> And Moses said unto his father-in-law, Because the people come unto me to inquire of God:
>
> When they have matter, they come unto me; and I judge between one and another and I do make them know the statutes of God, and his laws.
>
> And Moses' father-in-law said unto him, The thing that thou doest is not good.
>
> Thou wilt surely wear away, both thou and this people that is with thee: for this thing is too heavy for thee; thou art not able to perform it thyself alone.
>
> Hearken now unto my voice, I will give thee counsel, and God shall be with thee: Be thou for the people Godward, that thou mayest bring the causes unto God:
>
> And thou shalt teach them ordinances and laws, and shalt show them the way wherein they must walk, and the work that they must do.
>
> Moreover thou shall provide out of all the people able men, such as fear God, men of truth, hating covetousness; and place such over them to be rulers of

1

> *thousands, and rulers of hundreds, rulers of fifties, and*
> *rulers of tens.*
>
> *And let them judge the people at all seasons; and it*
> *shall be that every great matter they shall bring unto*
> *thee, but every small matter they shall judge; so shall it*
> *be easier for thyself and they shall bear the burden with*
> *thee. (Exodus 13:26)*

The foregoing counsel was given to Moses by his father-in-law, Jethro, who shortly departed from the Israelites to return to his flocks in the Sinai. Jethro was a simple herdsman, but a very wise man. His advice to Moses probably also makes him one of the first recorded organizational consultants. It is worth restating the seven principles of effective leadership set forth by Jethro, their religious overtones notwithstanding.

1. He advised Moses to resist micromanaging every situation that arises.
2. Moses was to "be . . . for the people Godward." In other words, he was advised to inspire and lead by example.
3. Moses was to establish the principles to guide the organization.
4. He was to clearly state his work expectations.
5. He was to choose able leaders who were people of integrity.
6. He was to delegate to these subordinates decision making appropriate to their ranks.
7. He was to intervene only in matters of great importance.

From the preceding, we can see that humans have known the basic principles of organization, management, and leadership for thousands of years. This book draws on the wisdom of the ages to illuminate modern approaches to the leadership of complex organizations.

Why yet another book on leadership, especially one that purports to draw on wisdom that in some cases is thousands of years old? This text looks at intrinsic leadership; that is, how to build leadership skills and how to apply them. To do this it draws on some "best and worst practices" from Western and Eastern cultures. The goal is to help readers learn *what* to do *when*, or how to conduct themselves in order to become the people who decide what to do when. Because great leaders and managers are generally people of action rather than words, many have left sparse written records. Those who have reduced their thoughts to written form, however, provide significant advice to modern managers. From the traditions of the West we have, for example, the thinking of Jethro as well as his eminence Cardinal Richelieu, who ran France and left an instruction manual for Louis XIII to follow after his death. We also have the teachings of Niccolo Machiavelli on power and manipulation, which should be understood by aspiring leaders but not emulated. The famous instructions of the Marquis of Pombal, Prime Minister of Portugal, to his brother on the occasion of the latter's assumption of his duties as Captain General of Brazil are also insightful, especially in matters of receiving counsel and making decisions.

From the Eastern tradition we have the excellent writing of General Sun Tzu and the *Analects* of Confucius. In addition, the biographies of great leaders are consulted for patterns of behavior that can be emulated. These include Napoléon Bonaparte, Fidel Castro, Dwight Eisenhower, Mohandas Gandhi, Martin Luther King, Jr., Abraham Lincoln, Douglas MacArthur, Admiral Horatio Nelson, Franklin Roosevelt, Pancho Villa, and others. To these are added modern theories of leadership illustrated with stories from the real world. The text also draws heavily from modern management theory.

Chapter 1 deals with the characteristics of leadership from the point of view of traits that are desirable in a leader and methods for their development. Chapter 2 explores human motivation and the appropriate ways to treat subordinates, superiors, and peers. Chapter 3 offers a leadership perspective on organizations, while chapter 4 focuses on decisiveness in leadership. Organizational communication is examined in chapter 5 through the framework of setting expectations and achieving desired outcomes through the use of power. The interplay of ethics and values as they pertain to leadership is covered in chapter 6. Chapter 7 focuses on leadership development for individuals and organizations.

This book is based on the premise that leaders are not born knowing how to lead. To be sure, they possess native intelligence, at least in so far as they are smarter than the average of the group they hope to lead. But analytic skills can be honed to razor sharpness. Great communication skills have been a hallmark of effective leaders. But history judges greatness as much by *what* leaders say as *how* they say it. The basics can be learned and applied to good effect. Much leadership literature tries to explain charismatic leadership. Possessing an aura that compels others to want to draw near and to suspend their personal judgment for that of the leader is a rare quality indeed. But even personal magnetism can be enhanced by the traits one exhibits and the manner in which one treats others. Personal integrity is a matter of socialization (how principles are learned and reinforced by experience) and practice (the manner in which individuals choose to apply their principles). Ethical leadership can be faked for a time, but the negative consequences of saying one thing and doing another are ultimately devastating for individuals and the societies in which they operate. Personal courage and steadfastness of purpose are traits that would-be leaders should cultivate in themselves and demonstrate by their actions.

In short, there is much that prospective leaders can work on internally. The importance of building relationships with others, particularly subordinates and superiors, cannot be overemphasized in a personal quest for advancement. Finally comes the matter of opportunities that define not only leadership, but greatness. Great leaders emerge amid or as a result of great challenges, whether such challenges are personally undertaken or thrust upon one by external circumstances. Lesser mortals in more ordinary times can look for advancement possibilities and seize opportunities as they present themselves.

The Nature of Leaders

> *And thou shalt teach them ordinances and laws, and shalt show them the way wherein they must walk, and the work that they must do. (Jethro to Moses, Exodus 13:26)*
>
> *The consummate leader cultivates the Moral Law and strictly adheres to method and discipline, thus it is in his power to control success. (Sun Tzu, 1988, p. 20)*

We begin with the vexing problem of defining the qualities inherent in leaders. To reduce the problem to its most basic terms, the leader is the one whom the followers follow. Conversely, the followers follow where the leader leads. This bit of self-evident tautology is often what we are reduced to when examining leadership. Why is one would-be leader followed while another is not? How did the successful one persuade the rank and file? What characteristics did he or she exhibit in the process and, of equal importance, to where was he or she steering the group? Moreover, was the group led or directed?

Traits of Leadership

Those who have studied the great leaders of the past to determine the reasons for their success have been frustrated when trying to determine a common set of traits that link effective leaders. What, for example, are we to make of physical characteristics such as height? The scriptures tell us that King Saul was "head and shoulders above the rest." Sam Houston stood six feet six inches in a society where the average man was five feet eight inches. George Washington, Andrew Jackson, and Abraham Lincoln too were well over six feet. While Saul, Houston, and company could be seen from the back of the crowd, the same cannot be said for Napoléon or Gandhi. Nor can great height explain the rise to prominence of leaders of middling height such as Douglas MacArthur and George Patton.

Integrity

The first quote at the opening of the chapter was part of Jethro's advice to Moses after the latter had become the undisputed leader of the Israeli people as designated by God. Sun Tzu, the great Chinese general of the 6th century BC, also spoke from a position of command. Most leaders lack the bona fides of a Moses and therefore come to their positions through a combination of their abilities, the group they seek to lead, and the circumstances with which the group is faced. Nevertheless Sun Tzu, whose writings have been studied for more than two thousand years by militaries throughout the world as well as those who aspire to be leaders, also recognized the importance of morality and steadiness of character in those who wish to lead.

Greatness in leadership, then, is associated with some ideal or principle that the leader teaches and inspires the followers to pursue. For Moses and Sun Tzu leadership was, in part, teaching followers to obey the moral law as they were given to understand it. The corollary is that a true leader must embody, not just teach, the principles that he or she wishes the followers to pursue. Moses and Sun Tzu both grasped this fundamental concept despite the fact that they emerged in two entirely different religious and historical traditions. Great leaders are uniformly considered to be persons of integrity by their followers. As used here, integrity means keeping one's promises.

> " A great prince should sooner put in jeopardy both his own interest and even those of the state than break his word, which he can never violate without losing his reputation and by consequence the greatest instrument of sovereigns. (Cardinal Richelieu, 1961, p. 102)[1]
>
> I do not consider it the act of a Prince not to keep his word to whomever he has given it. (Queen Elizabeth I, quoted in Chamberlin, 1923, p. 134) "

Of course, few who wish others to follow them do so by promising to be intentionally deceptive. Even sociopaths who are devoid of conscience pay lip service to honesty and fairness in their dealings with others. Western philosophy's most cynical viewpoint on this topic comes from Niccolo Machiavelli (1469–1527), whose advice to the Borgias, *The Prince*, has stood the test of time on how to manipulate power to sustain one's rule:

> 66 *Therefore it is unnecessary for a prince to have all the good qualities I have enumerated, but it is very necessary to appear to have them. And I shall dare to say this also, that to have them and always to observe them is injurious, and that to appear to have them is useful; to appear merciful, faithful, humane, religious, upright, and to be so, but with a mind so framed that should you require not to be so, you may be able and know how to change to the opposite. (Machiavelli, 1992, p. 81)* 99

Of course, this writer does not advocate Machiavelli's cynical worldview. It is mentioned to emphasize the importance of appearing to be honest as one seeks to rise in an organization. The easiest way to achieve the appearance of integrity, of course, is to conduct oneself with transparency and honesty. Real integrity means openly and candidly discussing issues with subordinates, peers, and supervisors alike; then, standing by one's pronouncements and actions. An honest opinion politely stated will serve uniformly well. When superiors decide against one's stated position, a person of integrity says "as you wish" and implements the decision to the best of his or her ability without seeking to undermine the authority of the superior. If, however, the decision involves organizational ethics, the person of integrity must decide whether to go along with the company line or resign. Over the long haul, acting with integrity will facilitate rather than hamper one's rise in the organization.

Intelligence

Intellectual traits are variable. Napoléon's skills at his lessons distinguished him with his instructors in military school, who then undertook to sponsor him with higher military authorities, thus advancing his early career. Abraham Lincoln (1809–1865) was said to be blessed with a nearly photographic memory and is celebrated as one of the world's greatest autodidacts. Lincoln had no more than a few years of formal education yet rose to greatness through self-study (he taught himself the law). His mastery of the language made him an outstanding communicator.

By contrast, though most presidential scholars consider Franklin Delano Roosevelt (FDR) to be one of our greatest presidents, he was a mediocre student at best. In assessing FDR's leadership qualities, a leading intellectual of the time observed upon meeting Roosevelt, "He has a second rate mentality but a first rate personality."[2] And, while Roosevelt (1882–1945) was athletic as a youth, the onset of polio in 1921 meant he had to win election and then govern from a wheelchair. (It should be noted that respect from the press resulted in FDR almost never being photographed in his wheelchair. It is therefore difficult to know just how many members of the general public knew about his handicap.)

In the final analysis, what seems to be true with regard to intelligence is that the leader of a given group need not be its brightest member, although he or she normally will be smarter than the average of the group. What seems to vary, particularly among political leaders, is just how far above the group average the leader actually is.

Charisma and Communication

What then are the traits that will cause those who are bigger or smarter to follow and sometimes revere someone who is clearly not their physical or intellectual equal? Sometimes called charisma, it is the possession of a special divine or spiritual gift that is sometimes known as the gift of grace. This gift has enabled some leaders to inspire not only their inner circle of followers, but the masses as well. If the scriptures are to be believed, this divine gift was the linchpin of Moses' ability to inspire his people. Though possessed of a speech impediment, he was able to convince Pharaoh to free his people (with several divine interventions) and to compel the people to follow him. After Moses' receipt of the law on the Mount, moreover, his countenance so radiated the power of God that it had to be hidden from the people, who could not bear to look upon his face.

The reasons for Napoléon's ability to inspire his troops and the populace of France are less divine in origin. Napoléon (1769–1821) was a Corsican, who thus spoke French with an Italian accent (not a good start). Convincing the French to follow him must have been based upon something more than his rhetorical skills. His military genius certainly was an asset. But the magnetism that he generated early in his military career when he displayed a reckless disregard for his own safety contributed greatly to his air of charisma. He would plunge into the enemy lines with sword slashing and return without a scratch, but with numerous bullet holes in his clothing. It was almost as if his enemies could not kill him, try as they might. In time, this air of invincibility and stories about it suffused his personality and reputation. But there was more to the man than that. Upon his return from Elba, he marched north at the head of loyal troops. The then-government of France, having no intention of welcoming him back, sent an army to stop him. When the two armies met, Napoléon presented himself to the hostile troops and, tearing open his tunic cried, "Who will shoot their emperor?" The opposing troops instantly burst into cheers and fell into ranks behind this remarkable leader, marching off to Waterloo where they shared in his ultimate defeat by foreign armies.

Charismatic leadership is often associated with communication skills through which leaders "sell" their vision. Adolf Hitler (1889–1945) was renowned for his ability to inspire his followers with ringing words of supposed shared truths. As his power grew so too did his ability to electrify the masses through carefully orchestrated rallies—complete with music, flags, uniforms, and lighting. All of this was designed to uplift and empower his followers through identification with their pride in the achievements of German culture in philosophy, music, and science. The theatrics and pageantry also tapped into the fundamental instinct to identify with the tribe or group. It is worth noting that people are not inspired by messages that make them feel more downtrodden than they already feel. Instead, charismatic leaders appeal to the righteousness of their cause, while negative factors are laid at the doorstep of others. They will often begin with a litany of complaints regarding the current regime or internal and external threats to the public. They end, however, with rousing exhortations aimed at lifting the spirits of the followers and inspiring them to act.

While Hitler was using his powers of persuasion to uplift the German people and to set them against their neighbors, on the other side of the world Mohandas Gandhi (1869–1948) was inspiring Indian nationalism through his message of self-determination, human dignity, and pride in things Indian and a rejection of English colonization. Gandhi's message was delivered without the use of trumpets, uniforms, or flags. Gandhi preferred traditional Indian clothing over Western business suits even though he was an attorney educated in England. Thus, his very appearance embodied the message he wished to send. His quiet spiritualism and "peaceful noncooperation"[3] plucked the crown jewel that was India from the British Empire.

Martin Luther King, Jr., (1929–1968) was able to inspire confidence through his ringing message of human dignity and the self-worth of his African American audience. King's message was delivered in the rhythmic cadence of a Black minister. His addresses were purposefully punctuated with biblical references such as "getting to the promised land" and "coming up out of Egypt." The quote below is extracted from Dr. King's speech at the start of the Montgomery bus boycott that launched him as a civil rights leader:

> *And we are not wrong; we are not wrong in what we are doing. If we are wrong, the Supreme Court of this nation is wrong. If we are wrong, the Constitution of the United States is wrong. If we are wrong, God Almighty is wrong. If we are wrong, Jesus of Nazareth was merely a utopian dreamer that never came down to*

> *Earth. If we are wrong, justice is a lie, love has no meaning. And we are determined here in Montgomery to work and fight until justice runs down like water and righteousness like a mighty stream. (Address to First Montgomery Improvement Association Mass Meeting, at Holt Street Baptist Church, December 5, 1955)*

King also had a broader appeal to the sense of justice of Americans in that what he asked of White Americans was no more or less than what the Constitution guaranteed: full equality and dignity before the law for every citizen.

Abraham Lincoln also demonstrated a great gift for articulating his worldview, both in his speeches and his writings.

> *A house divided against itself cannot stand. I believe this government cannot endure, permanently half slave and half free. I do not expect the Union to be dissolved—I do not expect the house to fall—but I do expect it will cease to be divided. It will become all one thing, or all the other. Either the opponents of slavery will arrest the further spread of it, and place it where the public mind shall rest in the belief that it is in course of ultimate extinction; or its advocates will push it forward, till it shall become alike lawful in all the States, old as well as new—North as well as South. (Lincoln's speech to the Illinois Republican State Convention, June 16, 1858)*

Lincoln was also possessed of a self-deprecating sense of humor and a great wealth of anecdotes, which he used to illustrate his point of view. Often to the frustration of subordinates, Lincoln would launch into a story that seemingly had nothing to do with the subject at hand but whose moral or punch line was exactly on point. When confronted with those with whom he disagreed greatly, he would often express his disagreement in a humorous way. Lincoln mocked his own military achievements in the Black Hawk War to make a point about the congressional opposition's attempts to puff up the record of another.

> *By the way Mr. Speaker, did you know I am a military hero? Yes sir, in the days of the Black Hawk war I fought, bled, and came away . . . It is quite certain I did not break my sword, for I had none to break; but I bent a*

musket pretty badly on one occasion. If Cass (the person being critiqued) broke his sword, the idea is he broke it in frustration; I bent the musket by accident. If General Cass went in advance of me picking huckleberries, I guess I surpassed him in charges upon wild onions. If he saw any live, fighting Indians, it was more than I did; but I had a good many bloody struggles with the mosquitoes, and although I never fainted from the loss of blood, I can truly say I was often very hungry. (Lincoln to the U.S. House of Representatives, July 27, 1848)

When Lincoln contracted smallpox, an aide asked if he should cancel the President's appointments with the legions of Republican office seekers. The President replied that by no means should the appointments be cancelled because he finally had something he could give them all (see Carman & Luthin, 1943).

Another president who vies with Lincoln for the title "the greatest" is the aforementioned Franklin Roosevelt. Born to the patrician class, FDR was said to be charming on an interpersonal level and a lover of good jokes and gossip. He was also celebrated for his ability to explain things to the masses in language they understood. He eased the minds of a dispirited nation during the Great Depression by assuring them that "we have nothing to fear but fear itself" (Roosevelt's First Inaugural Address, March 3, 1933).

In an act of true leadership, FDR went against the isolationist currents prior to American entry into World War II and announced his intention to continue to supply Great Britain with billions in war materials even though Britain indicated that it could no longer pay for them in cash (as prescribed by U.S. law). Roosevelt explained his clearly illegal proposal using the analogy of a garden hose.

Well, let me give you an illustration: Suppose my neighbor's home catches fire, and I have a length of garden hose four or five hundred feet away. If he can take my garden hose and connect it up with his hydrant, I may help him to put out his fire. Now, what do I do? I don't say to him before that operation, 'Neighbor, my garden hose cost me $15; you have to pay me $15 for it.' What is the transaction that goes on? I don't want $15— I want my garden hose back after the fire is over. All right. If it goes through the fire all right, intact, without any damage to it, he gives it back to me and thanks me very much for the use of it. But suppose it gets smashed

> *up—holes in it—during the fire; we don't have to have*
> *too much formality about it, but I say to him, 'I was glad*
> *to lend you that hose; I see I can't use it any more, it's all*
> *smashed up.' He says, 'How many feet of it were there?'*
> *I tell him, 'There were 150 feet of it.' He says, 'All right, I*
> *will replace it.' Now, if I get a nice garden hose back, I*
> *am in pretty good shape. (Franklin Roosevelt's Press*
> *Conference, December 27, 1940)*

Of course, FDR was planning to lend Britain (in addition to the garden hose) hundreds of warships and countless tons of munitions and other war supplies. This demonstrates true leadership in this author's opinion because FDR recognized the threat posed by the Fascist regimes and acted decisively despite the general spirit of isolationism and opposition to U.S. involvement in a European war (Burns, 2006).

Roosevelt also used the mass media (then the radio) to directly explain his policies and programs to the people during the Great Depression and World War II. Through a series of "fireside chats," he thus explained why banks were closing during the Depression. He also used this medium to galvanize public opinion in the wake of the Japanese attack on Pearl Harbor and the subsequent declaration of war by the U.S. Congress.

> *My Fellow Americans:*
>
> *The sudden criminal attacks perpetrated by the*
> *Japanese in the Pacific provide the climax of a decade*
> *of international immorality. Powerful and resourceful*
> *gangsters have banded together to make war upon the*
> *whole human race. Their challenge has now been flung*
> *at the United States of America. The Japanese have*
> *treacherously violated the long-standing peace between*
> *us. Many American soldiers and sailors have been*
> *killed by enemy action. American ships have been sunk;*
> *American airplanes have been destroyed. The Congress*
> *and the people of the United States have accepted that*
> *challenge. (Opening of Roosevelt's Fireside Chat*
> *December 9, 1941)*

Roosevelt's comments were not merely aimed at Japan. The "powerful and resourceful gangsters" included Nazi Germany and Fascist Italy. Roosevelt used the occasion of the Japanese attack on Pearl Harbor to justify a declaration of war against all three nations. Fortunately for Roosevelt, Hitler declared war on the United States, thus making it unnecessary to marshal public support for a declaration of war against all the Axis powers.

Leadership by Example

Not all communication is verbal. We earlier noted that Napoléon Bonaparte converted an opposition army that had been sent to destroy him by tearing open his tunic and demanding to know who would shoot their emperor. The historian Shelby Foote (1974) recounts that in the immediate aftermath of the American Civil War, an African American man entered an all-White church in Northern Virginia and knelt at the altar to receive communion while the stunned congregants sat mute. The onlookers remained in their seats until a lone figure came forward and knelt beside the man. That person was Robert E. Lee, whose actions far more than words conveyed his sentiments regarding post-war America. As a result of having commanded the largest Confederate army, Lee lost everything, including his military career and his home (taken to create Arlington National Cemetery). Yet he resigned himself to moving forward. Tragically for the nation, many other defeated Southerners lacked Lee's will to reconciliation.

The study of leadership must also account for the circumstances and events surrounding the actions of individual leaders. More often than not, history's leaders emerged on the scene when circumstances were favorable. In Hitler's case, the appeal of German nationalism came at a time when the German people were downtrodden by their neighbors, who insisted on the continuation of reparation payments for World War I regardless of their impact on the German economy. At the same time, the factional infighting of the Weimar Republic and the seeming fecklessness of German politicians also contributed to the strongman appeal of the Fuhrer (see Shirer, 1959).

Gandhi and the Congress party of India struggled through years of demonstrations, worker strikes, repression, and imprisonment until the Second World War so drained Great Britain as to make continued domination of the subcontinent impracticable in the face of stiff resistance. Unfortunately for Gandhi, Muslim and Hindu solidarity dissolved at the moment of independence (see Collins & LaPierre, 1997).

Martin Luther King's rise to prominence began with the Montgomery bus boycott that was sparked not by King but by the defiance of Rosa Parks, a mature Black woman who refused to give up her seat and move to the back of the bus in order that a White man might sit in the front (see Morris, 1984). It should also be noted that the larger American society was moving toward civil rights for African Americans. President Harry Truman desegregated the armed forces in 1948. The Democratic Party split in 1948 over Hubert Humphrey's keynote convention speech in favor of desegregation. In fact, a party platform that year spoke about the "fair deal" for all Americans. The Supreme Court unanimously struck down legally sanctioned segregation in schools in 1954 (U.S. Supreme Court, 1954).

The preceding examples are offered as context for assessing those who have come to be known as charismatic leaders. They each stepped forward and seized the moment to lead their followers despite great adversity and personal risk. Scholars who try to pin down charisma as a leadership trait find it easier to recognize than to describe. As we have noted, great leaders articulate a vision or a set of values with which their followers identify. The adjective *charismatic* seems to be attached in hindsight, when the leader is melded with the goals of the movement. He or she is thought to embody the values of the group and its goals. The messages they deliver, moreover, are overwhelmingly positive and designed to uplift and inspire, especially when the appeal is to a group that has been overlooked or oppressed.

Another feature of charisma is that it is rarely recognized beyond the person's followers. The World War II allied leaders recognized Hitler's charismatic powers but viewed them as a threat. Winston Churchill, often thought of as charismatic in his own right, called Gandhi a "naked faker." Certainly those responsible for the assassinations of Lincoln, Gandhi, and King were uninspired by them.

To summarize, there are common attributes that we associate with those whom we designate as charismatic. First, charismatic leaders seem to adhere to a highly developed set of personal principles. They also have the ability to articulate a vision for a movement or organization. They possess the ability to instill this worldview in their followers. This is done by using symbols and images familiar to their audience. In particular, the vision or mission that the charismatic person wants to instill is associated with reference points of the followers.

Successful charismatic leaders often find a solvable problem or an obtainable goal. They do not begin with the end state. Thus, Mahatma Gandhi persuaded the masses to make their own salt rather than to purchase that licensed by the British Raj. Elsewhere, he led groups of strikers in protests against working conditions and so forth. Reverend King set about desegregating transportation systems and campaigning for the right to vote. He did not undertake these missions everywhere at the same time. Nor did he insist upon complete nonnegotiable equality all at once. Lincoln's entry into the Civil War seemed almost measured when compared with the rhetoric and precipitous actions of the secessionist states. His deliberate response was to events that quickly spiraled out of control. Yet, Lincoln emerged from them more revered than before as the savior of the Union and the man who freed the slaves.

In more normal times when there is no imminent threat to the organization, leaders have more time to calculate their actions. Through consecutive small victories, these leaders build a sense of solidarity among rank-and-file members and help them achieve a great deal of collective and individual self-esteem. Simply put, one does not inspire one's followers by making them feel bad about themselves (see chapter 2).

Personal Courage and Commitment

Courage and commitment also seem to be integral components of the makeup of charismatic leaders. They see what must be done and proceed to act despite the misgivings of those who follow. And when adversity strikes, they show an amazing capacity for adhering to their goals although they are frequently willing to adapt their tactics. We have already noted the personal physical courage of Napoléon. Gandhi and King were able to face the prospect of imprisonment or worse with equanimity. Gandhi, King, and Lincoln all seemed to approach the possibility of assassination as a matter of destiny that was of much less consequence than the movement they were leading.

The attribute of personal composure at times of uncertainty and even physical danger steadies the followers and stiffens their resolve. Legendary Marine Corps General Lewis "Chesty" Puller (1898–1971) scolded officers for diving for cover when being shelled by the enemy. Puller would say "Don't do that (hit the deck), it makes the men nervous." Of course, whether lying or standing, everybody within a certain radius of a direct hit is assured of death or serious injury. But Puller seemed immune to the primordial impulse to duck that takes over the consciousness of most humans in times of danger. This disregard for his personal safety no doubt contributed to Puller's idealization as the embodiment of Marine Corps values and to his receipt of five Navy Crosses in his illustrious career as America's most decorated marine (see Hoffman, 2001).

Puller was a veteran of many battles, going back to the pursuit of the Nicaraguan revolutionary Sandino in the 1920s and 1930s. Puller realized that large-scale military maneuvers were ineffective for capturing or containing small, mobile bands of rebels. Puller's tactic was to create highly trained cadres of troops capable of living off the land and moving quickly through the Central American jungles. Puller never caught Sandino, but he kept him on the run to such a degree that Sandino could not organize and expand his movement to any effect during Puller's tenure.[4]

In the long history of Great Britain no hero is held in greater esteem than Admiral Horatio Nelson (1758–1805). Slight of stature, blind in one eye, and missing an arm from naval encounters, Nelson was an unlikely prototype for the dashing hero. His successful naval career culminated in his greatest victory at the Battle of Trafalgar, where he met his death. At Trafalgar, the British fleet engaged a numerically superior combined Spanish and French fleet. The British victory can be credited to Nelson's unusual and innovative tactics and the skill of British sailors.

Nelson deviated from the conventional tactic of lining his fleet up in a row facing the enemy and sailing past them in the opposite direction to exchange broadsides. This tactic allowed each combatant to bring all its guns on one side to bear and then—by coming about—employ the guns of the other side. Victory was often determined by the skill of the respective gun crews and the fortitude of the commanders and their willingness to continue. Just as likely, however, was that the side that had the advantage of the wind during the encounter would emerge victorious. Nelson was careful to add the advantage of the wind to his other advantages of tactics and skilled crews before attacking at Trafalgar.

In the battle, Nelson arrayed the British ships in a phalanx. He then sailed directly into the middle of the enemy line. The point of the British phalanx cut the lead French/Spanish ships off from those in the middle of the line. The lead ships of the French/Spanish line were at a complete disadvantage because they could not turn to assist their comrades in time to save them. Once the French/Spanish line was broken, the British ships surrounded individual enemy vessels and destroyed them (see Tracy, 1996).

Gandhi, King, Nelson, and Puller each displayed initiative and significant ability to initiate structures and tactics appropriate to the situation. They also led from the front—not asking more of the followers than they did of themselves. Gandhi, King, and Nelson died in the process. Gandhi was assassinated on his way to prayer. Dr. King was assassinated while in Memphis to lead a strike by garbage truck drivers. Lord Nelson was killed by enemy fire at Trafalgar. His last order to his crew was to cover his face so that the men would not know that he was dead.

"Chesty" Puller was not killed in action, although not from lack of putting himself in harm's way, whether in the jungles of Nicaragua or leading the marines' strategic retreat at Chosin Reservoir in Korea. In Korea, Puller was cut off from his supply lines in the dead of winter by the surprise entry of some 500,000 Chinese "volunteers" who crossed the Yalu river into Korea to reinforce their communist brethren. Surrounded and grossly outnumbered, Puller engineered a strategic withdrawal. He successfully fought his way to the sea and the shelter of U.S. naval artillery, bringing his wounded with him and destroying some seven Chinese divisions in the process. Because there was not enough room on the trucks for both the dead and the wounded, Puller took the time to bury the former in a mass grave before resuming the retreat. When asked by a reporter if the Marines were retreating he replied: "Hell no, we are advancing in another direction." This may have been technically true in light of the fact that before he turned there were more enemy troops behind than in front of him.

The achievements of the leaders noted above are the stuff of legends. None of these greats began their careers with a view to where events would eventually take them. None was born with the knowledge of how to lead others and remain steadfast in the face of adversity. On the contrary, skills develop in the course of a life's journey and are tested in times of adversity. Great events make for great humans. Greatness in response to challenges is a matter of hindsight. Getting large numbers of people to follow one's lead, however, is a prerequisite to success.

Skills to Be Cultivated

There are some basic skills that one can cultivate in order to prepare for leadership roles. One need not be born charismatic. In fact, most of those who history has designated as charismatic went through a developmental process, planned or not. So for those among us who are searching for ways to develop leadership skills without thought of becoming charismatic, there are some basic approaches that can be learned.

A Command Presence

Essentially, in times of stress effective leaders are calm, assured, and in control. These characteristics are conveyed to the rank and file through the leader's communication style, which does not involve yelling, threatening, or panic. Instead, leaders gather information and analyze it, often seeking subordinate input before deciding what is to be done. Orders are then given in a clear and precise tone so that followers have no doubt of the leader's wishes. Followers will also take cues from the leader's tone and manner. "Houston, we have a problem." This was how the commander of *Apollo 13* reported that his ship had an emergency situation that might result in the deaths of the three-man crew. From his tone one might have thought Mission Commander James A. Lovell was reporting a broken coffee machine rather than a critical systems malfunction.

When the stress of England's desperate situation in 1940 drove Winston Churchill to begin snapping at subordinates, his wife wrote him a note to remind him of one of his favorite sayings taken from the French: "One can only reign over souls with calmness (On ne règne sur les âmes que par le calme)." She went on to note: "Besides you won't get the best results by irascibility rudeness (sic). They *will* breed either dislike or a slave mentality—(Rebellion in war time being out of the question!)" (quoted in Meacham, 2003).

Grace under pressure is also conveyed by one's body language. Followers consciously and unconsciously study the leader for cues to how to react to the situation. Sitting on the edge of a chair and nervously adjusting clothing or drumming one's fingers on the desk do not convey strength or confidence. Likewise, nervously pumping one's leg under the table will be noticed. Effective leaders give the impression that they are accustomed to being in charge and to having their wishes carried out. As General Barry McCaffrey, the nation's most highly decorated four-star general, likes to say: "If you are in charge, for God's sake act like it." The comportment of Chesty Puller is illustrative of the point.

> *This was the man we were going to hear speak . . . not very tall, he stood with a kind of stiffness with his chest thrown out, hence his nickname 'Chesty.' His face was yellow-brown from the sun and atabrine, the anti-malaria drug that was used then. His face looked, as someone has said, as though it were carved out of teakwood. There was a lantern jaw, a mouth like the proverbial steel trap, and small, piercing eyes that drilled right through you and never seemed to blink. (Description of Puller by Brig. Gen. Edwin Simmons in Sutton, 1998)*

Puller's complexion was the result of his recent World War II service in the South Pacific. That notwithstanding, one would be hard pressed to describe Puller as anything other than a serious person with an exceptional command presence. Such a presence inspires confidence in the followers. By contrast, when a would-be leader exudes uncertainty and fear, the group will follow suit.

Other attributes commonly associated with superior leadership include high energy, enthusiasm for the task, purposefulness and perseverance—especially in the face of adversity, personal magnetism, organizing skills, concern for followers, and personal warmth.

Energy and Enthusiasm

Energy and enthusiasm are essential components for stimulating confidence in others and, more generally, for success in most of life's endeavors. One cannot inspire others to extraordinary efforts if one is personally incapable of such an endeavor. King Henry II, considered one of England's greatest kings, was remembered as a man who never sat down. Napoléon was said to have slept only four hours per night, a trait he shared with David Ben-Gurion, the father and early leader of Israel. Pancho Villa is said to have gone days without sleep and was so full of energy that he was constantly moving. Simply put, one does not rise to a position of leadership working the standard 40 hours per week. Energy and enthusiasm, moreover, must be manifested on the job. Leaving work early to go to the gym will not advance one's career no matter how strenuous the workout.

Purposefulness

A purposeful leader sticks to a path or position in the face of tremendous opposition. In sports, the leader rallies the players to rise up late in the game and literally "out tough" the opposition. Such people fight through their fatigue and urge their teammates to do likewise. Karate master Gichin Funakoshi, founder of Shotokan karate, put it this way: There are three important components that determine the victor in the contest; first is martial arts skills, second is physical strength, and third is fighting spirit. Of these three, fighting spirit is the most important (see Funakoshi, 1997). Purposefulness, looked at another way, is steadiness of purpose or moral courage—sometimes called the courage of one's convictions. Those whose behavior matches their unswerving commitment to their beliefs is much admired, even by their opponents.

Senator John McCain, for example, was offered an early release by his North Vietnamese captors because he was the son of a high-ranking navy admiral. Perhaps the North Vietnamese hoped that Admiral McCain would be positively disposed toward them, which could influence the Paris peace talks. The Vietnamese calculations did not take into account the resolve of then-navy flier McCain, who declined to be released ahead of other prisoners of war who had been held captive longer. He made this decision known in no uncertain terms, even though he was personally in need of medical attention. McCain did what he thought was right, knowing his decision might well lead to further torture and at the very least continued starvation and abuse. McCain could not have imagined the impact of this steadfastness on future political generations, who revere his steadiness of character whether or not they agree with his policy positions (McCain, 1999).

Of course, steadfastness, when carried to the extreme, can bring leaders and their followers to tragic ends:

> " Once the decision has been made, close your ear even to the best counterargument: sign of strong character. Thus an occasional will to stupidity. (Friedrich Nietzsche, 2000, p. 274) "

General George A. Custer was given to surprise attacks at sunrise as the best method of defeating the American Indians regardless of their number.[5] Thus, this charismatic hero of the Civil War ignored the advice of his Indian scouts, who reported that the Indian encampment they were about to attack numbered too many Indians to count. Custer also ignored the advice of his sub-commanders, who argued against dividing his forces. The result was the massacre of Custer and all the members of the Seventh Cavalry who were with him (including his two brothers) at what came to be known as the Battle of the Little Bighorn River (1876), in Montana (see Connell, 1984).

Personal Magnetism

Personal magnetism often is an indication of leadership potential. Some people exhibit a warmth of personality that makes others comfortable in their presence to the point that their peers just want to be with them. When leadership is called for, the group turns to this person for answers. Whether this quality is a product of endorphins, hormones, intellect, nurturance, or all of the above, some seem to possess it at a very early age.

An example of this phenomenon can be found in *Lord of the Flies* (Golding, 1962). In the novel, a group of preadolescent schoolboys is marooned on an island without adult supervision. As their circumstances become clear to them, they begin to organize and to think about what should be done. The smartest member of the group is a pudgy, bespectacled lad whom the others dub "Piggy." As the group ponders what to do, it is Piggy who articulates the need to build shelters, gather food, build a signal fire, and care for the younger children. Nobody listens to these ideas until another boy named Ralph says, "Piggy is right." The group then accepts the ideas and chooses Ralph as the leader—but, why Ralph and not Piggy? Is it Ralph's looks, his courage, etc.? This is what challenges scholars.

Organizing Skills

The most exhaustive look at leadership traits, known as the Ohio State Studies (Stogdill, 1957), attempted to list the traits common among leaders. The study's subjects were managers and its information source consisted of the managers' subordinates. The authors found precious little in the way of universal truths. The most effective managers, however, exhibited two distinct traits: a capacity to initiate structure and a concern for the well-being of their subordinates.

The capacity to initiate structure refers to the ability to define and structure one's role and the roles of subordinates toward achieving goals. Although this capacity seems to be a trait of effective leaders, many leaders of great movements have frequently relied on the organizational skills of others. For example, Gandhi had "iron man" Vallabhbhai Patel at his right hand. Patel organized members of the Congress party to participate in events and protests. He also worked diligently to provide Gandhi with personal security even though the latter rejected it. Patel was Gandhi's detail person, as were Prime Minister Nehru and others. When the independence movement came to fruition, Gandhi was thus able to transition into the spiritual leader of the nation.

For an example of a leader who possessed charismatic traits as well as inordinate organizational skills, the life of Pancho Villa is instructive. Born Doroteo Arrango in the late 1870s, the child of Mexican hacienda campesinos,[6] he took the name Pancho Villa after avenging an assault on his sister by one of the hacienda owners. Villa became a bandit and a cattle rustler while still an adolescent. Skilled at avoiding all manner of law enforcement sent to capture him, Villa ranged throughout the state of Chihuahua forming friendships and associations to support his life on the edge. Villa became a Robin Hood figure to the campesinos with whom he often shared meat and money. These relationships later formed the basis for his military organization, recruited from the ranks of campesinos, railroad workers, tradesmen, and former bandits.

Although he had virtually no formal education, Villa demonstrated masterful organization skills as well as personal magnetism as he rose to the rank of general during the Mexican Revolution. Organizationally, he created a logistics system for purchasing and transporting weapons and other materials from north of the border and a banking system to support his efforts and pay his troops. The logistical system also collected and dispersed food, clothing, blankets, and boots to his estimated 25,000 to 30,000 troops. Villa also displayed a knack for choosing able generals who were loyal to him and who possessed extraordinary courage, a gift for strategy, and battle skills. Finally, although the Division of the North[7] prided itself on its cavalry skills, Villa utilized railroads for the movement of troops and supplies in an unprecedented manner (Taibo, 2006).

Concern for Followers

As noted in the Ohio State Studies, the best managers exhibited concern for their subordinates. Often such leaders take an interest in subordinates that goes well beyond what is necessary to complete the work of the organization. Those who follow this counsel have been rewarded with loyalty and dedication well beyond the call of duty. Sun Tzu taught:

> *Regard your soldiers as your children, and they will follow you into the deepest valley; look on them as your own beloved sons, and they will stand by you even unto death. (1988, p. 52)*

To further illustrate the point, Chesty Puller ordered that in the field the troops would eat before their officers were served. When he wished to mail a letter or purchase stamps, he got in line with everyone else even though his rank would have allowed him to jump the queue. Finally, Andrew Jackson (1767–1845) acquired the nickname "Old Hickory" by walking back to Tennessee from a battle in Mississippi so that the wounded could ride. The act greatly endeared Jackson to his men (see Meacham, 2008). Fortunate indeed are the organizations in which leaders legitimately care for their followers.

Personal Warmth

Most successful leaders recognize that their followers are in awe of them and use this knowledge to their advantage in securing obedience. Those with extraordinary warmth, however, are special. Most leaders move through their organizations aware that those around them are highly attuned to their presence. On special occasions they make appropriate remarks and single out individuals for praise. They can be found moving through a crowd exchanging pleasantries and shaking hands here and there.

Those with exceptional personal warmth, however, seem to relish the opportunity to interact. They make eye contact and focus on the person to whom they are speaking as if he or she is the only other person in the room. They inquire about the person's health, job satisfaction, and family. For example, President Fidel Castro of Cuba is a master of public displays of personal warmth. Fidel, as he is known by ordinary citizens, will plunge into a crowd of Cubans, shaking hands and embracing people as if they were old friends. Often pausing to allow photographs, Fidel will put his arm around an old farmer and address him as *compadre*. Fidel physically touches and allows himself to be touched by the people. His security detail must have long since given up on protecting him from the people (see Ramonet, 2006). Two American presidents who exhibited the same sort of warmth for the people were Ronald Reagan and Bill Clinton.

Leaders with natural warmth display it more readily to their inner circle than to the larger society. They are quick to compliment subordinates for a job well done and go out of their way to thank those who put in extended hours on a project. More importantly, they take a real interest in the colleagues and subordinates as people. Franklin Roosevelt was on such good terms with the White House Press Corps that when a friendly reporter missed the presidential train, Roosevelt secretly wrote the man's column until he was able to catch up several days later (see Goodwin, 1994).

Personal warmth can be the stock and trade of politics even when the leader is not thought of as charismatic. Lyndon Johnson began his rise to power on his first day at the Capitol as a legislative aide in 1931. Johnson spent hours in the washroom feigning attention to his hygiene (shaving or washing his hands). He would introduce himself to other legislative aides as they entered the facility. When the association of congressional assistants met a day or two later, Johnson was elected its leader. Johnson went on to become Senate Majority Leader, Vice President, then President of the United States. But it was as a legislator that his personal gift shone most brightly. He was said to have known the names of every senator, their spouses, and children. He knew what school the member's children attended and how they were faring. If a senator's spouse was ill, Johnson would ask about her or him and offer his personal assistance, and mean it. It was his warmth that often convinced senators to support his legislation.

Unfortunately, his gift for interpersonal interaction did not extend to public speaking. Before a large audience or the television cameras he often came across cold despite his heartfelt language. In the modern era, presidents Kennedy, Reagan, Clinton, and Obama all had (or have) the capacity to project personal warmth through the medium of television. They could raise a crowd to its feet to cheer the message, or deliver a message that touched the hearts of television viewers. Presidents Reagan and Clinton proved particularly adept at healing the nation in times of tragedy, such as the crash of the space shuttle *Challenger* in 1986 or in the wake of the 1995 Oklahoma City bombing of the Alfred P. Murrah building.

So what are ordinary mortals who aspire to leadership to make of charisma, vision, magnetism, and personal comportment as they relate to their career development? First, as noted earlier, nobody is born charismatic or inspirational (the views of grandparents notwithstanding). There are leadership skills that can be honed and manners of personal comportment that can be cultivated. The remainder of this book examines these traits and skills in more detail and offers suggestions and examples that, in some cases, are thousands of years old. We turn next to motivation.

Notes

[1] Richelieu is perhaps best known as the Cardinal who was the foil of "The Three Musketeers" in the fictional novels of Alexander Dumas. He was, in fact, the ruler of France for many years during the unfocused reign of Louis XIII. As he sensed death nearing, he wrote a set of instructions for the king as a reference when he should no longer be there to offer advice.

[2] Attributed to Oliver Wendell Holmes, thought by many to be one of the most brilliant justices ever to serve on the Supreme Court.

[3] Called *Satyagraha*, this tactic involves refusing to comply with laws with which one disagrees, but it also requires acceptance of the punishment prescribed by the society for

disobedience. By peacefully going to jail, Gandhi and others in the Indian independence movement gained support within India and drew worldwide attention to the injustices of colonialism. Also, when the jails were full to overflowing, the British were left with no choice but to negotiate. Dr. Martin Luther King later adapted the tactics to the American civil rights movement.

4 The modern-day Sandinista Party currently in power in Nicaragua took its name from Augusto "Cesar" Sandino. Although now elected, in the 1980s the Sandinistas seized power, overthrowing the Somoza dictatorship that had been in power since the 1930s, much to the chagrin of the Reagan Administration.

5 The Cheyenne Indians under Chief Black Kettle suffered just such an attack from Custer earlier in his career that resulted in the deaths of many women and children. They therefore named him "The Son of the Morning Star." The Cheyenne were also present at the Little Bighorn.

6 In Villa's time, campesinos lived in a state of semi-slavery, much like serfs in pre-revolutionary Russia. They were consigned to a life of poverty and illiteracy. They were not at liberty to leave at will and had no resource in the law to remedy injustices by their overlords.

7 The Division of the North was so named to distinguish it from the southern revolutionary movement led by Emiliano Zapata.

Motivation

> ❝ *You will not succeed unless your men have tenacity and unity of purpose, and above all, a spirit of sympathetic cooperation. (Sun Tzu, 1988, pp. 63–64)*
>
> *The public often gave credit to Generals because it had seen only the orders and the result . . . that Generals won battles: but no General ever truly thought so. (T. E. Lawrence, 1991/1926, p. 584)* ❞

From the standpoint of leadership, motivation should be approached at the individual as well as the collective level. Chapter 1 addressed the role of leadership collectively with examples of great leaders who articulated inspiring visions in the language and symbols of their people. Leadership, however, also takes place at the micro level, where leaders seek outcomes from small groups and individuals. The discussion begins with some useful modern theories of motivation that are interspersed with ancient views. We then explore how to motivate individuals and groups.

Twentieth Century Motivation Theory

Two very different schools of thought dominated management theory in the second half of the 20th century. The first is generally known as **human relations theory** (see Herzberg, Mausner, & Snyderman, 1993; Maslow, 1987; McClelland, 1988; McGregor, 2005; Porter & Bigley, 1995). A central postulate of this theory is that human beings have certain intrinsic needs that they are trying to satisfy, particularly in their working lives. The second predominant theory of this time is **expectancy theory** (Vroom, 1964; Porter, Lawler, & Hackman, 1975), which seeks to understand the impact of incentive systems on worker motivation. The two overlap in that each is rooted in the perceptions of the workers. To illustrate this, consider the esteem need. Workers who feel that their contributions to the organization are recognized and appreciated in their working environment are thought by a human relations theorist to be motivated through the satisfaction of the esteem need.

Similarly, expectancy theorists judge the value of reward systems in achieving motivation in the context of the workers' perceptions. Thus, a worker who gets a raise and believes it to be recognition of his or her superior service will be motivated to do more, which in turn will result in higher productivity.

Other scholars (Steers & Porter, 1983) warn, however, that if workers learn that their own raise was less than another worker who is considered less than a peer, then the salary increase may well be a demotivator. The unifying factor in the two theories is that, regardless of the leader's intent, it is the perception of the workers that will determine how a particular incentive or organizational initiative impacts production (see Figure 2.1).

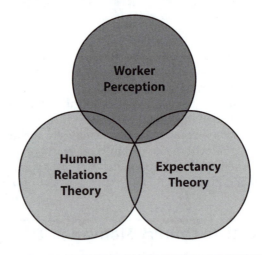

Figure 2.1   Twentieth Century Motivation Theory

There Are No Quantum Leaps in Organizational Change

Those who wish to become leaders, particularly those who wish to initiate organizational change, should be aware of the impact of the proposed change on the workers as individuals as well as their collective motivation.

Organizations do not move from point A to point Z without passing through points B, C, D . . . W, X, and Y. To ask them to do so is to invite failure. Change is often appropriate but rarely easily achieved. Having the vision to see that Z is possible and desirable is the stuff of leadership. Leadership is not possible nor is it necessary in the absence of goals. Conversely, sustaining the status quo can also be an act of leadership if the leader views sameness as a value and change as a threat to the organization. For example, the late Pope John Paul II expended a great deal of his considerable personal charisma resisting proposed changes to church doctrine such as the ordination of women. John Paul simultaneously increased the church's hierarchy by appointing cardinals who agreed with his views and altered and adapted church policy to reinforce the status quo. Whether adapting the organization to resist change or to embrace it, leaders can only advance change that rank and file workers are able and willing to implement.

Admiral Lord Nelson's victory over the combined French/Spanish fleet at Trafalgar was discussed in the context of leadership inspiration and innovative tactics in chapter 1. The victory was also the result of superior gunnery on the part of British sailors. Nelson recognized that the speed with which guns could be fired and reloaded was as important as the number of guns he possessed. Nelson therefore set about speeding up the process through repetitive drills until every gun crew in the British fleet could fire and reload in under three minutes. By contrast, other navies of that time took 9 to 12 minutes to reload. Thus, even though confronted by a larger fleet with more guns, Nelson had the advantage in firepower. It should be noted that Nelson did not begin the training with a demand for three minutes. Instead, he repeated the process over and over until the elapsed time was reduced from 12 minutes to 9 minutes and so forth until the goal was achieved.

The managerial legend Chester Barnard (2007) asserts that workers will comply with requests that they view as legitimate by virtue of the fact that they are trained throughout their entire lives to comply with authority in the form of parents, teachers, clergymen, and coaches. But, Barnard warns, if an order is considered illegitimate it may go unfollowed.

Barnard suggests that workers have what he calls **zones of indifference.** This is a perception range in which whatever is asked of them will be forthcoming with little to no resistance. This zone of indifference may be wide or narrow depending on the experience of the worker, the pressure she or he receives from the peer group, and the culture of the organization.

As long as the request is within the zone, it likely will meet with compliance. Radical departures from the zone, however, can prompt worker resistance simply because change is uncomfortable when compared with the status quo. For example, suppose a work group normally produces an average of 75 units of product in an eight-hour shift.

**Productivity Zone
of Indifference**

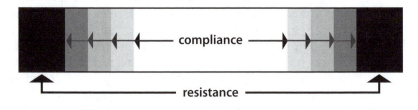

Figure 2.2   Productivity Zone of Indifference

Suppose further that this productivity level can be sustained without great exertion by a practiced crew and that the rate can be sustained without injury or production errors. The manager of this unit could instruct the group to push for 80 units per day with little resistance. Similarly, a modest slowdown to, say, 70 units per shift would not be resisted and might be welcomed by some. Management would be acting well within the zone of indifference.

On the other hand, abrupt announcement of a new performance standard of 125 units per shift would meet immediate resistance. Resistance could stem from workers' lack of confidence in their ability to meet the standard or from fear of injury or error from the speedup. The production increase might also be viewed as a management violation of the spirit if not the letter of a union contract. Worker resentment might result in an intentional slowdown, increased "errors," and multiple quality-control failures. More extreme responses might involve wildcat strikes (workers walk off the job without notifying management or the union leadership) or even industrial sabotage. Managers may anticipate this resistance even if they can demonstrate that other factories easily meet the 125-unit production standard.

Management rarely demands performance that is significantly below the zone of indifference. (Management theorists are thus excused from explaining this phenomenon.) Precipitous slowdowns nevertheless may be viewed as signs of eminent plant closings and the layoff of workers. These signs can raise worker anxiety, devastate morale, and send the best, most employable workers scurrying to find alternative employment.

Carefully communicating the need for production changes can go a long way towards easing workers' fear and anger. A true act of leadership, especially in a union environment, would be to engage unit workers in developing the new performance standards or methods, or involving workers in planning cutbacks that minimize the need for lay-

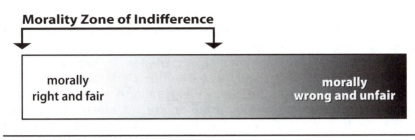

Figure 2.3 Morality Zone of Indifference

offs. This could include asking more senior workers to retire voluntarily to preserve the jobs of less senior workers.

Barnard (2007) also advises us that workers maintain a separate zone of indifference regarding morality. This "moral compass" is engrained in us from childhood and deals with right versus wrong and issues of fairness. So, suppose a supervisor asks a subordinate to trust that he really took an individual cab from an outlying airport to a convention center, rather than using the shuttle, but neglected to get a receipt for the cab ride that cost $25 more than the shuttle. "Please put through the reimbursement just this once." The clerk is likely to comply even though the exception violates a strict interpretation of the company policy. The request probably would not activate the morality barometer of most accounting clerks. Repeated requests, however, would probably result in a refusal to comply because the clerk would be pushed beyond indifference and because an auditor would question the clerk's personal competence and fiduciary reliability. More importantly, repeated requests for exceptions would be viewed as a violation of organization policy and fundamentally unfair to other workers who took the trouble to get receipts.

No matter how necessary or desirable change might be, rank-and-file workers must identify with the change or, at the very least, not feel threatened by it. Whether applied to change or preservation, leadership involves translating one's vision into concrete terms that followers can understand. Martin Luther King used biblical analogies to reach his followers. Terms like "deliverance," "coming up out of Egypt," and "making it to the promised land" resonated with his followers.

Leadership requires converting the goal into concrete actions that move the group toward objectives that the leader has articulated. In Dr. King's case, transportation boycotts, marches, and lunch counter sit-ins were used to dismantle the Jim Crow laws that defined American apartheid. The overarching goal was a color blind society with full economic, political, and social equality for all. Change was achieved in jurisdiction after jurisdiction. Dr. King's efforts were further aided by the fact that he was not asking for changes that were outside the zone of indifference of the greater society. That is, American society on the whole accepted equal justice before the law as a fundamental tenet. So, despite the resistance the movement experienced in local segregated jurisdictions, what King sought was what the Constitution promised. The speed with which *de jure* (by law) segregation was abolished would have been slowed considerably if the Southern Christian Leadership Movement had demanded set asides in employment for the previously disadvantaged or special consideration for admission to universities at the outset of its efforts. To this day, such demands still fall outside the zone of indifference of many Americans.

Inspiring People to Change

Convincing a society or an organization to depart from the status quo requires an expansion of the zone of acceptance in a positive direction, but how? As early as the 1930s, the literature of management began incorporating the lessons of behavioral science into its prescriptions for effective organizations. That is, a central component of organizational change involves the attitude of workers, so how can we motivate them to perform better?

Beginning in the 1930s with the Hawthorne Experiments, led by Elton Mayo, management theorists came to realize that worker attitudes could be as important to productivity as organization discipline and equipment (Gillespie, 1991; Mayo, 2003). Ironically, the Hawthorne investigators did not set out to measure worker motivation. Their intent was to vary the work environment to determine factors that could have a positive impact on productivity. What they learned was that it mattered little whether the assembly line was sped up or slowed down or whether the lighting was brightened or dimmed. In every case, productivity increased. When questioned, the workers indicated that they felt the company cared about them and they wanted to do their best to please. Note that the motivating factor was the perception of employees who individually and collectively viewed management as more caring. It was not a matter of expectancy or the gratification of some intrinsic motivation.

In the decades that followed, the human relations school of management identified various factors that seemed to motivate workers. Both Maslow and Herzberg, for example, theorized that higher order need gratification was necessary to maximize worker contributions. These included:

- *Recognition* of one's efforts by the organization.
- The sense that one was held in high regard (*esteem*) by the organization.

• Providing the individual worker with interesting and challenging work that allowed him or her to *self-actualize*.

Whether recognized as basic by enlightened management or forced upon them by organized labor, organizations seemed to provide for lower order needs as identified by the theorists. These included sufficient pay to sustain the worker and his or her dependents and a sense of job security along with a safe work environment.

Porter and Bigley (1995), in their attempt to operationalize Maslow's theory, identified the need for *autonomy* as a prerequisite for higher order need fulfillment. People need the autonomy to plan their work in order to be innovative or creative. Autonomy is difficult when all one's work activities are an extension of the supervisor's will and orders can change from hour to hour through the day. Porter and Bigley therefore concluded that higher order need gratification was impossible for the bottom two-thirds of most organizations. But wise managers have long known that kindness, caring, and recognition are rewards in themselves. Cardinal Richelieu (1585–1642) advised Louis XIII in part that:

> The late king (Henri IV), your father, being in dire extremity, paid with kind words those who served him, accomplishing with caresses what his lack of funds would permit him to encourage by other means. (Cardinal Richelieu, 1961, p. 41)

Confucius presaged the Cardinal by a couple thousand years:

> Rule over them with dignity and they will be reverent; treat them with kindness and they will do their best; raise the good and instruct those who are backward and they will be imbued with enthusiasm. (Confucius, 1979, p. 65)

As the events related in the box on the following pages indicate, esteem, autonomy, and basic respect can be significant motivators for workers in the lowest, dirtiest occupations society has to offer.

A Tale of Two Managers

"You cannot punish them harshly before they love you." (Sun Tzu)

In the mid-1960s, a rich field of asbestos was identified in the California coastal range. A major asbestos manufacturer commenced operations using engineers/managers sent from headquarters and production workers recruited from the job pool of the nearest town, some 25 miles from the mine. The opening of the mine was viewed in the small town as an economic plus. Local politicians saw it as a step toward diversification of an economic base that was reliant on agriculture and a decreasingly productive petroleum field. Working-class immigrants from the South and Midwest welcomed the opportunity for steady work at real wages.

At full capacity, the manufacturing process was as follows: The asbestos was scooped from the earth using bulldozers and skip-loaders that dumped it into a large tumbling dryer. There, the large rocks were separated from the lighter dirt and asbestos. The latter materials were then sent into the mill where they were passed through a series of shakers with increasingly fine screens until the asbestos material was separated completely from the dirt. The asbestos product was then passed through a grinder that ranged from powder to fluffy depending on the end application of the product. The mill environment was filled with white dust. Clean-up at the end of a shift involved workers blowing the dust off their clothing with a high-pressure air hose.

Construction and initial management of the plant had been entrusted to a senior engineer highly skilled at start-up operations. The engineer's interpersonal style was such that upon being introduced he would shake hands firmly and say, "call me Merle." He wore no tie and his safety helmet gave testament to many close encounters with solid overhead objects. His most striking feature, however, were his hands. They were big and powerful and bore the marks of one who had started at the bottom. When approached with production concerns or suggestions, Merle would listen patiently, ask questions, and either authorize experimentation or explain why this or that would not work.

The mill building was constructed by contractors, but installation of mill equipment was handled by the first cohort of employees who eventually became the production crew, whose foreman we shall call Ivan. Ivan had been hired because of his years of experience working with machinery in the petroleum industry.

Merle's management style can be illustrated by his handling of a rush order that arrived on a Friday afternoon. He drove 25 miles to the mill (which had no phone service), arriving at 4 PM, just before quitting time at 4:30 PM. He told Ivan to have the men shut down the noisy bagging equipment and gather around. Merle explained that he had a rush order for 1,000 bags of a particular grade of asbestos but there were only 700 bags of the product in the warehouse. "Now, I figure it will take about 5 hours to bag the other 300 bags and load the lot on the trucks. You can do it tonight or we can do it on Monday. You all can decide. But, because today is the end of the pay period, I went ahead and wrote down 5 hours of overtime on your timecards. If you decide to wait 'til Monday, just give me a call when you get to town and I'll remove the inch-and-a-half (overtime) from your timecards. It's up to you boys. I have to run." Merle then left the crew to decide. When he reached the exit, he turned back toward them and added: "Oh, by the way, I thought you might be hungry so I bought you all hamburgers and milk shakes. They're on the table in the break room."

Clearly, Merle's preference was to get the order out immediately, but he left the production decision to the crew. It is not surprising that the crew decided to stay and do the job. What is interesting is how they did it. Instead of eating first, four of the crew members set about producing the needed 300 bags. The remaining five members, including Ivan and the lab technician, loaded the other 700 bags into the tractor trailer that would deliver the materials. The crew then swept the entire mill and lubricated all the equipment. The work was completed in just over three hours. The cold hamburgers and melting shakes were consumed on the hour-long bus ride from the mill into town. The only unhappy person in the process was the shuttle bus driver, who had to wait three hours for the crew.

Shortly after these events, Merle completed the hiring of four full crews of workers and the mill was put into operation on a 24-hour, seven days a week basis. Once things were running smoothly, Merle was succeeded by two operations managers. The workers were sorry to see Merle leave, but his talents were needed elsewhere.

Enter the X-Men

The new operations managers were a very different breed from Merle. They seemed to subscribe to the Theory X philosophy put forward by Douglas McGregor (2005).This view postulates that workers are unmotivated, incapable of initiative, and that they will seek to avoid responsibility at any opportunity. A wise manager therefore keeps a close eye on the workers. The two new managers are referred to hereafter as the X-men. The X-men viewed the manufacturing process as simple and the tasks rather routine, requiring little in the way of complex decision making from rank-and-file workers. The X-men subscribed to the beliefs that production quotas are to be rigorously enforced, equipment must be maintained, the mill must be cleaned regularly, and workers must provide a day's work for a day's pay. Adherence to these principles guided most of the X-men's decisions. Unlike Merle, the X-men were not receptive to suggestions. When approached with suggestions or questions they were apt to reply, "Do it that way because I said so." Or, when questioned, "Trust me, I'm an engineer."

Furthermore, they insisted on maintaining a social distance from the workers appropriate to their status in the hierarchy; this formality, combined with their control needs, was a formula for disaster. The X-men spent their days at the mill checking production records, giving orders to shift supervisors, and sneaking about trying to catch "nonproductive workers." When the X-men were in attendance, the workers did their level best to comply with management expectations. Those workers not engaged in bagging product or testing ore samples busied themselves sweeping floors and lubricating equipment. No matter, the X-men knew in their hearts that the workers could not be trusted.

The rift between management and labor became complete one day when Ivan instructed two line hands to accompany him to the upper storage facility to bring down a 55-gallon barrel of glue for the asbestos sacks. Halfway to the stor-

(continued)

age facility, the three were surprised by the senior X-man, who brought his pickup to a sliding stop and demanded, "Where do you three think you're going?" When Ivan explained their purpose, the X-man cynically quipped, "I suppose the three of you are going to carry that drum down the hill." Ivan patiently explained that the skip-loader from the dryer was meeting them to haul the barrel to the mill. "There is no need to take the skip-loader off-line, I'll drive you myself. Hop in," he said. The two younger workers nimbly sprang into the bed of the truck while Ivan opened the passenger side door. "No! No!" the X-man exclaimed, "you ride in the back with the other help." He could not have done more damage to his relationship with Ivan and the two stunned workers if he had struck Ivan in the face. A clearly embarrassed Ivan struggled over the side of the pickup bed while the two workers averted their eyes. The battle lines were drawn.

The workers knew that the X-men would not arrive at the plant before 9 AM because of the distance from their offices in town and the necessity that they be available by phone to the east coast headquarters. Furthermore, they had to leave the plant by 4 PM to arrive at the office in time to complete their own paperwork requirements. Once they started down the hill, moreover, there was no place for them to turn around for at least 5 miles. When the taillights of the X-men's pickups disappeared around the first turn, the workers were liberated.

Little changed on the day shift, but, at 4 PM when the taillights disappeared around the bend, the games began. It turned out that, by slowing the belt just a little, three men could approximate the work of eight, with a little bridging effort by the whole crew toward the end of the shift. While three worked, five played cards or slept in the break room. Then, some of the crew members began taking judo lessons. The stacked bags made an excellent soft-landing surface upon which to practice their throwing techniques. Of course, nobody removed their boots, which resulted in a number of broken bags. The evidence was concealed by dumping the contents of the broken bags into the recycle vent in front of the grinder. The practice had the added benefit of incrementally increasing the crew's production numbers for the shift due to the injection of finished product.

During the rainy season, production had to be slowed because the ore from the saturated ground was too wet to dry. The plant then operated on reserve materials stored in huge bins behind the plant. Productivity was further slowed because the warehouse was reaching its capacity due to the inability of the eighteen-wheel trucks to climb the rain-saturated dirt roads.

Thus the bored mill hands developed a sports competition dubbed the "Asbestos Olympics." The mill and warehouse were laid out in the shape of a large L. The competition involved pointing a forklift loaded with asbestos toward the opposite end of the warehouse. Bets were laid on who could give the forklift the greatest head start (measured in seconds). The machine would be put in motion without a driver. The runner's task was to wait the prescribed interval then dash out the mill door and reenter the warehouse at the other end in time to stop the forklift before it crashed into the wall or the stacked bags of asbestos.

The record was five seconds. The champion was a skinny Louisiana fellow named Jack who bet that he could beat the machine with a seven-second head start. (It should be noted that the previous record was set in dry weather). Undaunted by the pouring rain or the darkness of the midnight shift (and bolstered by the fact the Ivan was in the break room and unlikely to interfere), bets were laid and the race was on. Some argued that Jack had taken off before the allotted time had elapsed. That complaint was forgotten completely as Jack traveled barely ten feet before falling on his back in the slick mixture of mud and asbestos. His wager partners were so doubled over with laughter that they neglected to turn off the careening forklift. The result was the destruction of several tons of asbestos product including the full pallet of product on the forklift and several others that were stacked against the wall.

Needless to say, Ivan was not amused. But his personal loyalties to the crew and his dislike for the X-men overcame his supervisory tendencies. He decided to cover up the incident for all their sakes. The plant had to be shut down completely and the broken bags run through the recycle vent before the day shift and the X-men arrived in less than three hours. The recycling was the easy part and the product was quickly repackaged in new bags. The crew's dilemma was how to dispose of the asbestos-coated broken paper bags. They could not be put in the overflowing garbage bins. Fortunately, the plant kept an ample supply of diesel fuel on hand for the earthmoving equipment. The broken bags were hauled some distance from the plant, through the pouring rain. Then, gallons and gallons of diesel fuel were applied creating a bonfire that illuminated the mountains for miles around.

The crew's one mistake in covering their tracks was that they neglected to reset the bagging-counter that the X-men used to monitor the production of each shift. "The counter doesn't lie," was the X-men's response to any shift foreperson who dared to make excuses for a sub-par shift output. That night, Ivan's crew set the single shift record for the number of bags produced in eight hours. Not surprisingly, the X-men could never reconcile the counter totals with the number of bags in the warehouse. They were seen wandering in the warehouse for days, clipboards and slide rules at the ready.

Three months later the mill was unionized by a near unanimous vote of the workers. Ivan and his crew eventually went on to other jobs. Thereafter, turnover continued to be high. Some blamed the commute, others the boring work, and some the unhealthy working conditions. A few even blamed the treatment they received from management. None of these complaints, however, had ever been voiced when Merle was running the plant. The plant closed after a few years as a result of various asbestosis-related litigation. (Indeed, several members of Ivan's crew either died or experienced serious respiratory problems as a result of their brief employment at the mill.)

As the asbestos case study illustrates, it is possible to provide workers with a degree of autonomy and, more importantly, respect—even in the most mundane production environment. And, as the X-men learned to their chagrin, systematic disrespect for worker dignity and intelligence is a formula for failure and perhaps unionization of the workforce.

> ❝ . . . *a man who attacked a child would be blamed by everyone. In similar fashion, I make bold to say, a great king should never insult his subordinates since they too are relatively weak. (Cardinal Richelieu, 1961, p. 41)* ❞

No matter how seemingly informal the work environment is, managers should not forget that they are in a superior position and are therefore responsible for setting the tone for relationships with workers. Smirking, snide asides, and disempowering condescension are all too common in workplaces where, ironically, the managers insist on being called by their first names.

Returning to Chester Barnard's description of the zones of indifference, these are particularly relevant for the novice manager wondering how to get workers to follow instructions. The reality is that we are socialized—beginning with our mothers—to give authority figures what they ask. We know further that adult workers find work as natural as play and, rather than shirk responsibility, they will seek it under the right circumstances (McGregor, 2005).

Middle-aged workers in particular will insist upon the autonomy to do their jobs without being micromanaged. What motivational theorists hope to convey is that workers seek fulfillment and pride in the tasks that they perform. Looking over their shoulders while they work or attempting to entrap them doing something wrong is a surefire formula for rendering them immobile. Worse, they may engage in us-against-them behaviors that can destroy an organization's productivity

What should be clear from Barnard's analysis is that those seeking to motivate workers must understand the culture of the organization, the established norms for productivity, and the enthusiasm of the workforce for the task at hand. They may then begin their initiatives for the organization from the standpoint of where the organization *is* rather than from where they presume it should be. An organization whose mission has been in place for a number of years during which leadership has not changed, will fall into routines that become enmeshed with worker expectations. Changing those routines or reorganizing the preferred lines of communication will inevitably lead to organizational stress. Reducing this stress is the responsibility of the leader, who should clearly indicate the path he or she wishes to follow and the steps that should be taken. First and foremost, a leader must convince those in the leader's inner circle of the wisdom of his or her plans and the specific responsibility that each subordinate is expected to undertake. By working through subordinate leaders, change moves outward from the inner circle through middle managers and first-line supervisors.

Those who want to lead well should realize that people near the bottom look to those immediately above them for cues on how to react to orders. Returning to a military example, rank-and-file soldiers look to their noncommissioned officers (NCOs) for guidance. NCOs not only share fox holes with privates but also the risks that might follow from ill-conceived orders. If the sergeants accept the order and follow through quickly, so will the troops. Had the X-men earned the respect of Ivan and his cohort of shift supervisors, they could have avoided countless problems in the production process.

When communications from above are not clear and lines of authority are overlapping, the end result will be a workforce that is confused and dissatisfied. This can cause two immediate negative consequences. First, change will be carried out in a chaotic and stressful manner, if at all. Second, the change agenda may displace the central components of the organization mission with no significant progress toward either end.

> *When the general is weak and without authority; when his orders are not clear and distinct; when there are no fixed duties assigned to officers and men, and the ranks are formed in a slovenly, haphazard manner, the result is utter disorganization. (Sun Tzu, 1988, p. 53)*

At bottom, those whom one would motivate must also be given incentives to work beyond the intrinsic value of the task at hand. This is particularly important when a leader is trying to motivate subordinate supervisors and managers, who in turn must motivate their subordinates to achieve the desired outcomes.

> *Requisites for getting the most out of subordinate managers: The first is that Your Majesty have confidence in them and that they be aware of it. The second is to require them to speak freely and assure them that they can do so without peril. The third is to reward them liberally so that they will believe that their service will not be without adequate recompense. This is especially necessary because there are few men who love virtue naked. The fourth is to empower and support them so openly that they are assured of no need of fearing either the artifices or the power of those who would try to destroy them. (Richelieu, 1961, pp. 62–63)*

Managers perform their best when they are certain that their leader has confidence in them and when that confidence is expressed regularly and publicly. Subordinates also function better when they may speak freely about their organizational concerns without fear of retribution.

66   *. . . there are few men who love virtue naked.*   99

Workers do their best when they are paid appropriately. This is particularly true in the public sector, where scholars long ago realized that the best way to defend against corruption is to set a standard of high ethics and to compensate government employees sufficiently so that they are not tempted to take bribes (Weber, 1946). Furthermore, modern public organizations are beginning to adopt systems of bonuses for those who successfully carry out the organization's mission. Finally, Richelieu notes that it is critical for managers to back their subordinates, openly and publicly, and thereby imbue their actions with the authority of the leader.

To this point, we have presented leadership behaviors that have engendered motivation and others that have proven to be de-motivational. We turn now to the issue of individual motivation.

Individual Motivation

Most people are willing to meet basic performance standards of the organization because they have been taught to do so since childhood. The process begins in infancy, when parents are most responsive to babies who smile. Indeed, parents and others spend hours trying to coax smiles from infants. Babies who lack these intimate interactions as a result of parental neglect or from being raised in institutions have difficulty forming attachments and finding fulfillment as adults (Oppenheim & Goldsmith, 2007).

Fortunately, most people get the early nurturing that they need and proceed to childhood, where parents, teachers, and others reward cooperation and compliance. As a result, adults enter organizations with the ingrained knowledge that giving authority what it wants is the path to reward or at least the path of least resistance. The groundwork is therefore laid for those who presume to give orders.

Unfortunately, "one size fits most" approaches give short shrift to the experience that individuals bring with them. Those entering the workforce bring reference points taken from parents, teachers, and other significant persons from their childhood and adolescence. More seasoned workers bring their past work experience and reference points that may or may not have been positive. For example, one worker might have been downsized out of his or her previous job after years of promises of job security.

Another may have been in the same position for 30 years with little hope for advancement. A third might be a single parent of three who needs job security and health care benefits. The variety of reference points held by individuals is highly idiosyncratic. Nevertheless, as long as expectations are within the zone of indifference, compliance need not be a worry.

Staying within the zone of indifference is as easy for those who merely wish to manage as it is for those who wish to lead. This difference is more than semantic. As one observer put it, "Managers do things right, leaders do right things" (Bennis, 2003). Managers occupy positions of authority within the organization and are given responsibility for achieving organizational outcomes. Managing well is facilitated by authority vested in them by the organization and by general social norms that insist that authority be obeyed. Managers are given authority to establish work plans, supervise and discipline individuals, and to exercise signature authority for the allocation of resources. (If one lacks signature authority, one is a supervisor—not a manager.) Therefore, a manager of middling abilities who meets the expectations of higher ups may anticipate a trouble-free career.

Leaders do much the same thing as managers. The distinction is that leaders look for ways to improve performance and output and are able to persuade and inspire rank-and-file workers to push themselves to achieve the leader's vision. Most of us are familiar with internal slogans, group meetings, and so forth that tout the values of excellence. Beyond these, there is the matter of individual motivation.

Talk to Them

Mary Booksin was Director of Nursing at a state mental health facility for children and adolescents. In addition to her nursing degree, she possessed a master's degree in management. She was often referred to by her social worker colleagues as well as the nursing staff as "By the book Booksin," due to her insistence on record keeping and treatment documentation. These were part of her obsession with meeting all state regulation and hospital accreditation standards.

Mary was perplexed when she received a phone call from the Executive Director of the facility. It seemed that the new Commissioner of Mental Health was intent upon making his agency the premier mental health system in the region in the near term and the entire country over the long term. He intended to do this through motivated and committed employees. Employee turnover was antithetical to his plans and the Commissioner did not like the turnover numbers he was seeing in the facility. A meeting was scheduled.

Mary entered the meeting with a look of cordiality tempered by tolerance for the "headquarters" people, who managed from afar seeing only the big picture. The delegation was led by the Deputy Commissioner of Mental Health, who began the meeting by saluting the facility for its recent reaccreditation. This was the first time in many accreditation cycles that a site visit team did not find major problems

(continued)

with the record-keeping function. "You understand the Commissioner's concerns that you perform so well in this area, yet seem unable to reduce turnover."

Mary smiled and explained the seeming anomaly by noting that turnover was primarily among technicians rather than the professional staff. "I am not satisfied with most of the applicants who might be seeking long-term employment in low-paying jobs. Because we are located in the same town as the State University, I am able to recruit bachelor's- and master's-level students. They come from the school's programs in clinical psychology and psychiatric social work. They work here while pursuing their degrees. They receive their degrees in either December or May, thus our turnover occurs in January and June. The decision to trade turnover for competence is a conscious one for which I take full responsibility."

There followed a moment or two of silence, during which the HQ staffers checked the numbers and nodded their confirmation of Mary's version of turnover. The Deputy Commissioner chuckled and then asked, "Are there any other innovations you would like to share with us?"

"Well, if you're really interested, I have three," Mary replied. First, she always made sure to staff the quality assurance committee with several psychiatric technicians. She also made sure that the committee met on a monthly basis to review records. "That way, I am able to turn quality assurance from a cumbersome chore into a vehicle for achieving excellence."

"Second, I converted several full-time technician positions into part-time ones to facilitate staffing a 24/7 organization. The only downside is that it means more work for the scheduler. Third," she reported, "we recently started several program enrichment initiatives that include physical fitness and art therapy." Mary noted that these initiatives were accomplished without busting the budget. She then offered them a tour of the facility.

In the commons area between the children's and adolescent's dormitories were located a series of weight-training devices, all of which were attached to the wall and appropriately padded for safety. Mary explained that the equipment was an excellent venue for burning off excess energy, especially when the weather prohibited outside play. "The weight-training equipment is only used under the close supervision of the psychiatric technician who installed it." Mary went on to explain that the technician in question was a competitive power-lifter who worked at the hospital to provide health care benefits to his family while he trained for competitions.

The art therapy room was a converted double office just off the commons area. It contained various artist materials, and the walls were decorated with a variety of artwork that ranged from stick figures to highly sophisticated drawings. Mary explained that the technician who ran the art therapy program was a trained artist who worked at the facility to support his family while he pursued his art. His job enabled him do what he loved.

"Most impressive," the Deputy Commissioner remarked. "But how did you pay for all of this when none of it appears in your budget?"

"That's where I come in," said the facility director. "I have started a foundation to help support our efforts here. I am happy to report that all of this equipment was paid for by private contributions."

"Most impressive! But, I have one last question. How did you identify the technicians who had the special talents?" asked the Deputy Commissioner.

"Why, I just talk to them," Mary said.

"I just talk to them." This simple formula can unleash a flood of creativity and organization loyalty, if the person in authority will but find the time and inclination to relate to subordinates on an interpersonal level.

This book's author once undertook a survey of the clerical workers at the university where he worked. After some standard data analysis, he was able to classify them into five categories. The one common feature across categories was an overall high level of job satisfaction.

One group was primarily motivated by fulfillment of security needs. Another cited good pay and benefits. A third expressed a positive work environment as their incentive for remaining. The fourth, and by far the largest group, expressed the view that they liked their job because it fit their lifestyle. They noted that work schedules were flexible so they could take their children to the doctor or pick them up after school. The overriding motivation for this group was the flexibility of the university schedule, which permitted them to take time off work around holidays and to work a flexible schedule during the summer. Free tuition and the opportunity to attend classes during working hours was the motivator for the smallest group in the study. Several in this group had more than one bachelor's degree and one had obtained a master's degree. Significantly, none of the 300 plus respondents had received a raise in two years.

The supervisors of the archetypes for each group were asked to rate the job performance of their secretaries. One department chair called his secretary, an older woman named Wanda, the best secretary he had ever had or ever heard of. When asked to describe her ideal job, Wanda responded, "A retirement check." Asked why she put so much effort into her job she said, "Because everybody has to work. So, you might as well do your best while you're at it."

The most revealing interview for this author was with his own part-time secretary, who was the archetype of the flexible schedule group. She reported that she worked because she needed the money. She chose the university because the alternative was a commute to "the city" some 20 miles away. When asked about her relationships at work she said, "It's an okay place." "Just okay?" the author asked. "Well, you all are nice enough and make jokes and stuff but nobody here cares about me, not really. You don't care about my life or my kids and stuff, but, like I said, it's okay." The interview triggered an introspective look at himself as a manager/leader. He was friendly and informed and always spoke to everyone, but obviously needed to talk to his secretary like Mary talked to her technicians in our case study.

Emotional Intelligence

Daniel Goleman (2006) significantly advanced the field of organizational studies when he identified what he called **emotional intelli-**

gence. The crux of the matter is that emotional intelligence is not measured by IQ tests or academic achievement. Rather, it is a set of skills and sensitivities that enable one to work effectively with others. It is characterized by the aptitude for reading people and situations and formulating appropriate responses. This aptitude involves sensitivity to others, particularly the ability to perceive one's effect upon them. Those with high emotional intelligence seem to empathize with others and to adapt their conduct, especially their language, accordingly. There are five elements to emotional intelligence theory, one of which is a characteristic of all leaders: namely, motivation or a strong drive to succeed. The remaining four elements are far more interesting from the standpoint of leadership dynamics.

The first is self-awareness, or the ability to recognize and understand one's moods and emotions and their impact on others. The second is self-regulation, or the ability to redirect one's disruptive impulses or to suspend judgment of others. Another is empathy, or the ability to understand the emotional makeup of other people and to identify with them and adapt one's behavior accordingly. Fourth is social skills, or the ability to find common ground with others.

Perhaps the most universally useful component of emotional intelligence is self-awareness. When leaders understand their own moods, feelings, and needs they are better able to control themselves and to offer up responses that are consistently socially acceptable and which achieve the desired ends. Furthermore, those high in emotional intelligence will examine situations after the fact and make adjustments in their personal response style when similar situations arise. Suppose, for example, that an individual has a tendency toward flippancy. That is, he or she might respond jokingly and dismissively when important matters are raised. Or, perhaps, they are flippant when another is honestly expressing an uncomfortable emotion. In both cases the flippant individual may actually be expressing personal discomfort with the conversation. The flippant remark in times of gravity may reflect an effort to seem cavalier in the face of stress. Similarly, the quick wisecrack in an emotional situation might be an effort to minimize the other person's discomfort as well as one's own by quickly cutting off the strain of the situation. Unfortunately for the joker, she or he may be taken as a person who lacks sufficient gravity to warrant being entrusted with serious responsibilities. A flippant response to a statement of concern can make one seem insensitive, uncaring, or just plain stupid.

Similarly, people with a tendency toward quick anger and harsh words must limit this type of response if they hope to one day rise in the organization. Anger toward the weak, especially in an unequal power situation, is more likely to evoke fear than to inspire frankness, cooperation, or compliance.

> *Anger makes dull men witty, but it keeps them poor.*
> *(Queen Elizabeth I to Sir Edward Dyer)*

People with high emotional intelligence are characterized by the ability to listen to the concerns of others and to formulate an appropriate response that minimizes the harmful impacts on the listener. At the very least, they are able to avoid repeating the mistake through self-examination and self-control. Former Senate Majority Leader George Mitchell had a reputation for measured responses and an empathetic personality. Mitchell reports that he honed his skills carefully. He explained that he would go home each night and go over the day's events. He would review in his head various encounters, particularly those that had gone badly. He would then try to identify alternative approaches that he might have used to achieve a better outcome. Such was his reputation that, after leaving the Senate, his name was regularly mentioned for an appointment to the United States Supreme Court during the Clinton years. Ultimately, he was appointed to mediate a peace accords in Northern Ireland, which he did successfully. The result was a shaky but continuing peace and Nobel Peace Prizes for factional leaders but not Mr. Mitchell (Hoge, 1998). Most recently he led the inquiry into the use of performance-enhancing drugs in major league baseball (Schmidt, 2008). It is hard to judge which of the latter two imbroglios required the most emotional intelligence to bring about a result acceptable to all concerned.

A consensus expert on emotional intelligence was the American founding father Benjamin Franklin (1706–1790), who always seemed to contain his discontent in favor of consensus making. The skill sustained Franklin through years of public service that included a stint as the representative of the Commonwealth of Pennsylvania in England. Franklin also was an active participant in building the consensus that led to the Declaration of Independence. Perhaps his greatest achievements were as leader of the U.S. delegation to France.

While in England, Franklin's great intellect, personal warmth, and sense of humor enabled him to create for himself a social network of scientists, philosophers, noblemen and women, and members of the parliament who were sympathetic to the cause of the colonies. Franklin sustained his equanimity despite the reality of constantly running into a stone wall with the Crown and parliament over colonial rights.

As the representatives of the various colonies debated how to proceed, the Second Continental Congress was torn apart between those who seemed to want to appease the Crown through petitions for redress of grievance, and those who pushed for independence. Through it all, Franklin's jovial low-key approach deflected the anger of his opponents and acted as the voice of reason among the radical, whose cause Franklin favored. The result was the Declaration of Independence and a united front against continued association with Great Britain. In France, Franklin's diplomacy, wit, and charm at court secured French support of the American Revolution in the form of loans and war materials, not to mention a sizable French fleet and a considerable number of French troops (Isaacson, 2003).

This self-taught master of interpersonal relations always chose reason and restraint over anger and confrontation when pressing his case. Franklin devised one of the most useful techniques for persuading others to his point of view. He developed the skill while serving as the representative of Philadelphia in the colonial legislature. When confronted with a colleague who was disposed to oppose his position, Franklin would not attempt to bargain with the adversary or proffer gifts or promises of a *quid pro quo*. Instead, Franklin would ask a favor of the person such as the loan of a particular book. Franklin would read it quickly and return it promptly, in mint condition. He would then engage the loaner in a dialogue on the ideas set forward in the book, which would often result in an agreement between Franklin and his policy protagonist. Franklin would thank the person profusely for the loan and offer to return the favor in the near future. In so doing, Franklin would establish himself as a well-meaning and thoughtful colleague. This made it much easier to approach the person regarding Franklin's policy preferences. Although it never appeared in *Poor Richard's Almanac*, the aphorism "Sell yourself first, then sell the product," might have headed his list of ways to succeed in life. In Franklin's case, the self-sale was often initiated by asking a favor from the other, a truly unique approach.

In summary, those with high emotional intelligence seem to conduct themselves flawlessly in stressful situations. They are adept at defusing tension and finding a middle ground between antagonists in organizations. This suggests that emotional intelligence is innate, much like native intellectual ability. Also like native intelligence, emotional intelligence can be honed through education and practice. Unfortunately, social science has not yet figured out how to measure emotional intelligence as precisely as it does IQ. Nevertheless, the impact that individuals with high emotional intelligence have on their subordinates, peers, and superiors in organizations is undeniable.

It also seems abundantly clear that emotional intelligence is singularly lacking in the predator species. Tigers and sharks go about their business with no regard for their victims. So too do organizational predators who seem to lack empathy in their single-minded pursuit of power and self-advancement. Organizational predators seem incapable of registering the impact of their behavior on others. Or at least they don't seem to care. A negative response to an overbearing behavior is viewed as lack of understanding or weakness on the part of the recipient. Training in emotional intelligence for such predators would offer no more than another technique of manipulation. Recall the words of Machiavelli from chapter 1:

> *Therefore it is unnecessary for a prince to have all the good qualities I have enumerated, but it is very necessary to appear to have them. And I shall dare to say this also, that to have them and always to observe them is injurious, and that to appear to have them is useful; to appear merciful, faithful, humane, religious, upright, and to be so, but with a mind so framed that should you require not to be so, you may be able and know how to change to the opposite. (Machiavelli, 1992, p. 81)*

Unfortunately, the ability to read others, to appear to empathize with their feelings and to alter one's tone and manner of expression accordingly is the stock and trade of unscrupulous used-car salespeople and sociopaths as well as empathetic managers. Followers do well to fine tune their own emotional intelligence skills to avoid the honey-baited traps of false prophets.

Returning to the discussion of the leader as motivator, what is important to note is that our behavior and affect are as important as our words when giving instructions to subordinates. High performance employees, whether motivated by a desire to please or merely to do a good job (à la Wanda), will respond badly to mercurial behavior by supervisors. Ordinary workers and low performers can readily be made fearful by emotional outbursts. It is not unreasonable to assume, moreover, that when threatened with discharge they will either provide the minimum level of performance or leave the organization. In either case, the problem of nonperformance is minimally solved. It is wishful thinking, however, to believe that bursts of anger and berating subordinates will yield high-level performance. Such behavior by managers invariably falls well outside the zone of indifference of individual workers.

3

Organizational Structure

" *. . . thou shall provide out of all the people able men, such as fear all the people, able men, such as fear God, men of truth, hating covetousness; and place such over them to be rulers of thousands, and rulers of hundreds, rulers of fifties, and rulers of tens. (Exodus 13:26)* "

Human knowledge about organizing complex human collectives reaches back through the ages. Returning to the advice given to Moses by Jethro, the lessons to be taken are as follows: First, large diverse organizations have complex problems that range from organizational vision and direction (God's instructions and which way to the Promised Land?) to mundane problems such as fodder for the herds, who shall camp where, or where to find toilet paper in the desert.

Once a critical mass is reached, somewhere in the neighborhood of 25 to 30 members, the tasks of management become too complex for one individual. To succeed, the leader must be *able* to delegate decision authority to subordinates. The word *able* is emphasized in the previous sentence because leaders are frequently unwilling to rise above day-to-day problems and come up with systemic solutions, as was the case with Moses. In modern organizations, managers sometimes get bogged down in mundane operations, leaving for tomorrow what is not due today. Workers thus find themselves pulling all-nighters to finish important reports that sacrifice quality to the exigencies of deadlines.

Those with a great deal of confidence in themselves and who have achieved a measure of success in lower echelons of the organization often advance due to their own innate abilities, capacity for hard work, and attention to detail. While these are laudable traits and are certainly necessary to achieve notice by superiors, they should be supplemented with an ability to assess others and appropriately delegate authority. Just as important to success as being able to delegate is what the Ohio State studies identified in the 1950s—the ability to initiate structures to manage recurring tasks (Stogdill, 1957).

The parameters of delegated authority, however, must be clearly specified. The failure to draw specific lines can result in a failure to act on the part of those who are reluctant to give orders on their own initiative. Of equal danger are those who zealously exercise their authority and often overstep their mandate, which can at times undermine and displace greater organizational goals.

Furthermore, as suggested by Jethro in the opening passage, those who are to exercise subordinate authority should receive their appointment on the basis of demonstrated competence and their ability to command the respect of subordinates. One of the most revolutionary concepts offered by Confucius was the principle of advancement based on merit rather than hereditary kinship. Appointments based on kinship, friendship, or cronyism, while scoring high marks for loyalty and gratitude, can rarely duplicate the abilities of the leader. Napoléon learned this to his chagrin by appointing relatives to exercise authority over conquered lands (see Asprey, 2001; Landau, 2006).

Lincoln too learned this difficult lesson when he was forced to appoint political cronies sponsored by radical northern politicians rather than competent bureaucrats to administer the government procurement process in the Civil War (Carman & Luthin, 1943). The result was a great waste of taxpayers' money, a slower than necessary Union mobilization, and a resultant prolongation of the Civil War. In the final analysis, many a charismatic leader has learned that friendship is no guarantee of loyalty; furthermore, affability does not equal competence. Cuban revolutionary Fidel Castro learned this lesson with regard to the appointment of ministers:

> **❝** *One should not have confidence in someone simply because they are a friend. (Castro, quoted in Ramonet, 2006, p. 99)* **❞**

This is so because self-interest and naked ambition often cause persons appointed through interpersonal connections to turn on their sponsors. Task competence and shared vision are much better appointment criteria.

Task competence seems obvious at first blush. But, as noted earlier, competence at one level does not perforce predict competence at the next, especially if the duties and responsibilities shift. Worth noting in this regard is how few star athletes go on to excel as coaches. The ranks of the latter are generally populated by those with sufficient athleticism to play the game well, but who also are able to rise above their individual position skills and understand the strategic interrelationships among various positions and the overall goals of the team. They also display a knack for motivating individual athletes to broaden their personal skills and to coordinate their performance with others. Unfortunately, excellence in interpersonal leadership skills does not translate into automatic technical competence in making complex organizational and financial decisions. Ernesto "Che" Guevara proved himself to be a dynamic, fearless leader of one of the three revolutionary guerilla columns in the Cuban revolution. Che also proved himself an absolute disaster as a finance minister in the new government (Taibo, 1996).

Talented leaders observe their subordinates for signs of strategic thinking, a willingness to take initiative, and demonstrated ability to get others to follow them. Such potential can be converted into leadership through nurturance and support.

The second criterion of **shared values** is one of the most overlooked factors in the organizational literature. Simply put, subordinates are most likely to perform well when they agree with organizational goals and have confidence that the leader shares these values (Sperlich, 1969). Many public sector professionals choose their careers precisely because they value the ends of public service (e.g., schoolteachers, social workers, and public safety professionals). Convincing them to work for the values inherent in their agencies and career choices is not as difficult as might be the case in organizations whose initial common linkage is profit.

The Role of Hierarchy

Whether ancient or more modern, traditional organization theorists questioned the ability of leaders to manage and direct the activities of more than a few subordinates (Fayol, 1949; Thompson, 2003). The optimal reporting system is five to seven subordinates per supervisor. This narrow span of control performs two functions. Beginning at the top, the various echelons relay instructions and coordinate activities downward through the lower tiers of the organization. Conversely, the system reports problems and concerns up the hierarchy. Information, in this model, is on a need-to-know basis. The goal is to narrow the focus at each descending level so that those near the bottom need hardly think at all. Their task is to obey rather than question. Questions slow the process and may displace the intent of those in command. Answering questions also delays action and undermines good order and discipline. An axiom for military career success is, "Don't ask questions above your pay grade." One may, however, ask for clarification of "what" is being ordered and, when in exceptional circumstances, "how" something should be done. The rank and file are not at liberty to ask, "Why are we doing this?" "Good order and discipline" have been the watchwords for military success through the ages. Even today these hierarchies largely remain in place. The army recruiting slogan, "an army of one," refers to individual training that allows the soldier to adapt to changing situations rather than permission to question the mission.

Rigid hierarchies work best in an atmosphere of harsh and certain discipline. The Chinese sage and general Sun Tzu (1988) reported on the sad necessity of having to summarily execute a brave soldier who took the liberty of charging the enemy line and quickly dispatching several of the enemy before returning to the cheers of his comrades. He was executed for acting without orders. Fortunately, such extreme discipline is not permitted in most modern organizations, thus mitigating the efficacy of strict hierarchies. (The obvious exceptions to this are authoritarian dictatorships, criminal enterprises, and terrorist organizations.)

The Downside of Hierarchy

In the middle of the last century, organization theorists began to question assumptions regarding the appropriateness of rigid hierarchies in a variety of situations. Some questioned the basic assumptions of the model regarding its ability to achieve required outcomes and to honestly pass information up and down the organization pyramid, concluding that organizations should be as flat as feasible (Drucker, 1998). In fact, with regard to the flow of information, the opposite is equally possible: that various echelons may act as filters for orders coming down the pyramid, especially when they view an order as counterproductive or antithetical to their personal interests. Conversely, those in the middle may be reluctant to pass information upward, especially when it reflects badly on them.

The advent of computer technologies, especially e-mail, has dramatically reduced the need for humans to pass information up and down the system. Efficiency of messaging notwithstanding, an overreliance on technology has the potential for decimating the middle ranks of organizations. Their exit from the organization is accompanied by a loss of institutional memory and problem-solving skills. Their absence can result in problems left unsolved from lack of expertise, or problems may swamp senior officials in the manner of Moses. That said, the downsizing of organizations in recent years has often focused on middle managers.

An additional challenge to hierarchy is information interpretation. This can occur at each echelon as data are collected and synthesized before being passed up the chain. Thus, for example, an intelligence officer responsible for reporting on enemy activity in his province would review reports from subdistricts. Suppose there were four such reporting districts, three of which reported limited to no enemy activity and one noting significant activity. The report might reflect a 75% pacification. If the scenario were repeated for the entire nation, commanders might believe that they were winning the hearts and minds of the people when in fact the enemy was massing for an attack.

Precisely such errors were made in the Vietnam War in advance of the Tet Offensive in January 1968, when American commanders were surprised by a nationwide enemy attack. Even though enemy casualties outnumbered American casualties more than ten to one and the offensive virtually wiped out the Vietcong structure of South Vietnam, the offensive is considered the turning point in American public opinion about the war, eventually leading to an American withdrawal (War Library, 1988).

Information failures due to hierarchy in civilian organizations are rarely as dramatic as the Tet Offensive; nevertheless, communication networks that rely strictly on hierarchical reporting systems can result in unanticipated consequences and a slowing of organizational progress. This is especially the case when initiatives in one branch of an organization require the understanding and cooperation of other divisions. For example, the Office of Personnel Management (OPM) of a midwestern state sought to implement a new system of electronic testing by which potential employees could apply for state jobs and take the exam at any branch of the Department of Employment Services. A work group was formed that included external computer programmers and the OPM's most knowledgeable employees. The timeline for project development was rigorously managed with the result that the technical system was ready to be put into operation on schedule. Unfortunately, no one in the various agencies, including line personnel at OPM, knew how to work the system, or even knew that it was coming. The result was an implementation delay of over a year. Much of the delay and confusion could have been avoided by a system of inter- and intra-organization communication about the program, including training for those who would be using the system and the beginning of hardware installation during the latter days of program development.

Factors Influencing Structure

Variables beyond leader assumptions of human motivation and traditional organization assumptions also act as determinants of appropriate organizational structures. Miles (1975) suggests that variations in organization *mission, environment,* and *technology* should also drive the design of operating systems. To these should be added the element of *organizational culture.* Leaders who recognize these factors can turn them toward their own ends.

Mission

Organization missions can range from fixed to ambiguous. Workers at a steel mill, for example, need not ponder the mission at the beginning of each shift. Their job is to manufacture steel. How much to produce and where it will be shipped are management decisions. In these circumstances, a traditional hierarchy is applicable.

Conversely, a software development company may find its mission changing along with consumer demand, the activities of competitors, and developments in its own work product. Work groups engaged in the creative or developmental process must establish working modalities that facilitate and encourage the free exchange of ideas and information. Therefore, a collegial approach is most appropriate. Contributions from work-group members are essential to product development. Creativity is maximized when members view themselves as part of a team collectively responsible for defining and achieving the mission. Creative teams frequently define the mission, develop operational plans, and hold themselves and each other accountable for achieving specific milestones in product development. Issues of rank and hierarchical deference are secondary to maximum interaction and cooperation. Thus a culture of informality is formed that is confusing to the uninitiated.

For example, a retired marine lieutenant colonel with a computer background was initially at a loss as to how to conduct himself when he was hired by a computer manufacturer to work in the product development division. According to the colonel, it was several days before he could identify who was in charge of his work group. Everyone was addressed by their first name and individuals felt free to interrupt one another in discussing work much like one might find in a discussion of football strategies in a sports bar. There were no private offices and the indifference to fashion was equal among all the engineers. It took some time for the colonel to be socialized into this new and strange culture.

In some organizations, the mission has never been rigorously defined or questioned. In such cases, the necessity of setting priorities may seem like a bother to the rank and file. But, the worst case scenario is when structures are thrown into place to deal with complex challenges without clear delineation of decision authority or functional responsibility.

Ill-defined missions are not the exclusive purview of private companies. Examples of such neglect are also commonplace in government. An example of mission ambiguity in government is the war on terror, where cooperative effort among law enforcement and intelligence agencies is more appropriate than large-scale military operations. Rigid communications hierarchies and narrow foci are not conducive to interagency-intergovernmental information sharing. Nor is it feasible to develop coordinated responses to impending threats when hierarchies are in place. The problem is multiplied when we consider the necessity for international cooperation among nations with varying degrees of democratic development and a variety of ideological values.

Task forces. The middle ground between hierarchies and informality is known as the task force approach. It is particularly useful when cross-agency or division cooperation are essential to completing a mission. Falling midway between hierarchy and collegiality, the task force allows public or private organizations to deploy resources and personnel on an ad hoc basis to resolve a mutually pending problem. Task force members work on the problem at hand with the expectation that they will return to their normal duties at the end of the operation. Of equal importance is the fact that task force members must retain their identity with the parent organization to which they will ultimately return and to whom they are also accountable for their actions on the task force.

In effect, they are the representatives of their base agencies, which will continue to command their primary loyalties. Task force members can only cooperate to the extent permitted by their base organization superiors. The most effective task forces, therefore, are those in which high-level executives have committed to outcomes. For example, if the chief executive officer of a for-profit enterprise maintains a close watch on the task force, then interdivisional cooperation will follow. But executive indifference can lend itself to game playing by division leaders even though their task force representatives are committed to cooperation.

The centrality of high-level commitment is amplified when the task force is inter-agency or intergovernmental. Intelligence agencies will share information to the degree that they perceive such sharing as being in their self-interest or when the task force activities are regularly accountable to top political executives.

Most organizations routinely function somewhere between the hierarchical model and the task force approach, depending on the decision to be made and the level of resources that must be brought to bear on a problem. Involving workers in problem solving, moreover, enhances organization commitment and can lead to innovative solutions that may not be self-evident even to the most gifted manager.

The threat of empowerment. The problem of worker empowerment is perplexing for those reluctant to delegate decision making for fear that their authority will somehow be diminished. They should understand that most workers are aware of the reality that "having a say differs from having a vote" (De Pree, 1989, p. 25). Leaders must, however, balance the benefits of subordinate inputs with their own sense of the problem at hand and the appropriate steps to be taken. Those at the top of the pyramid are presumed to have the widest possible perspective and they are expected to exercise good judgment for the benefit of the organization and its stakeholders. Private sector managers have a fiduciary responsibility to protect organization assets and provide shareholders a return on their investment. Failure to do either can lead to devaluation of the company's stock, which would ill serve investors and rank-and-file organization members. Public sector managers have a similar responsibility to elected officials and to the public at large. Public managers are expected to consume resources prudently and to act as guardians of the public interest.

Whether they work in the public or the private sector, leaders are expected to exercise their own best judgment in both daily problem solving and planning for the long-term well-being of the organization. In the final analysis, the participatory leader has the task of maximizing creativity through participation without ceding his or her own best judgment to the group-think process.

Managers who trust their subordinates to engage in good faith problem solving are normally rewarded by enhanced commitment to the organization and increased personal loyalty—natural outgrowths of mutual respect and consultation. Bringing to bear multiple perspectives also has the potential for maximizing the options available to the organization as well as decreasing the likelihood that unanticipated problems will arise from choosing one alternative over another.

Perhaps of equal importance is to find an admixture of consultation and formality that the individual leader is comfortable with. In this regard, the middle ground can work quite well in most situations.

Managing from the Middle Ground

One of the most effective managers in this author's experience was a city manager who gathered as much information as possible from his subordinates, decided what needed to be done, then gave instructions publicly. When important matters came before him requiring cross-unit coordination, he would assemble his various department heads for a discussion. He would lay out the problem as he saw it and ask for each member's view of the impact on his or her department. He would also individually and directly solicit input from them as to problems or implications of various solutions. In this process he would ask if he had missed anything or if the proposed solution might cause additional problems. When he was satisfied that he had sufficiently explored the matter, he would give specific instructions to each manager.

Worth noting is that every manager was expected to apply his or her best judgment to the problem at hand. They were free to disagree, albeit respectfully, and they were delegated to perform specific tasks for which they would subsequently be held responsible. This city manager had been at the same medium-sized city for nine years. His two predecessors had lasted less than two years each. His longevity probably owed a great deal to his using the same consultation strategy when dealing with the city council members, with whom the manager consulted individually regarding needed changes in the city's government and the impacts of those changes on council districts.

Environment

The decision-making framework a leader must utilize shifts more and more to the environment as one's career progresses. That is, the manager's attention from the middle on up an organization hierarchy is characterized by less and less focus on operations and internal environments and more focus on the organization's external environment. At the apex of the organization, the preponderance of an executive's time is taken up with the environment. Leadership is the successful steering of the organization through an environment that ranges from stable to turbulent.

Environmental variations about which prospective leaders should be aware include the state of the economy, actions of competitors, demands from the consumers of organization products, and so forth. Traditional factors in the environment include current and potential clients, current and potential competitors, and the development of alternative production technologies (Porter, 1998).

Adaptation and Organization Survival

For years the treatment of alcohol and drug addiction used the 12-step social model, which traditionally meant a 28-day inpatient treatment regime followed by years of follow-up help from support groups. The advent of managed care, however, forced treatment providers to reexamine their treatment modalities and delivery systems. Under managed care, insurance companies contract with treatment providers to deliver services at a fixed rate. Profitability requires that the insurance company work to keep costs low by pushing providers to prescribe generic drugs. They also press physicians to forego unnecessary tests and to minimize inpatient stays.

Managed care companies demanded a more flexible treatment system involving shorter inpatient stays, admixtures of inpatient and outpatient treatment, and so forth. Treatment providers were faced with the decision of whether and how to adapt to this new reality. One strategy would be to fight the change and attempt to convince the insurance companies to reverse themselves. Alternatively, providers could decide to move to a private pay model in which they would only take clients who could cover the cost out of their personal resources. Some moved to provide combinations of inpatient and outpatient delivery systems and to coordinate with referring professionals for the aftercare needs of their released clients. Treatment providers who recognized the new reality and tried to adapt their treatment modalities were faced with the necessity of convincing their rank-and-file workers that a new mixed delivery system could be accomplished without sacrificing treatment quality. Those that adapted have thrived and grown. Those who did not turned into boutiques for celebrity clients or went under.

Environmental factors are also critical in the public sector. Local managers who wish to introduce new approaches to solving societal problems are faced with the realities of the political climate in which they operate. Problems such as air pollution, urban water quality, and transportation challenges require interorganizational cooperation and the combining of political as well as financial resources.

Creating a Light Rail System

In California, for example, new taxes require a two thirds vote of the people. So, transportation planners seeking to reduce urban traffic congestion by creating a light rail system had the task of convincing both elected officials and the citizenry to support the initiative. In Santa Clara County, an alliance among various local politicos, career managers throughout the county, and nongovernmental organizations used a countywide strategy to convince weary commuters to vote for the project. Their efforts were helped by the fact that voters in the county had a history of providing the needed super majorities for initiatives that were both necessary and explained in a systematic manner. Selling the program was aided in no small part by the fact that the Board of Supervisors was led by an advocate for rail transportation.

At a more theoretical level, governments are influenced by the management theories that are in vogue in their environments. During the 1990s, for example, a movement to streamline government services swept the nation. At the national level it was called the *new public management* and was led by then Vice President Al Gore. At the state and local level, the new public administration, as envisioned by Osborne and Gaebler (1993), led to an outsourcing of many public services. Government leaders were convinced that any reduction in government would save money and be welcomed by tax-weary voters. Services such as waste management were contracted out, reducing government payrolls and their accompanying expenditures for health care and public employee retirement benefits.

The hoped-for cost savings to government often did not materialize as anticipated because waste management companies must negotiate union contracts with their drivers that include health care and retirement benefits. These costs are passed on to the contracting unit of government. In this example, public policy makers who correctly read an environment adverse to taxation failed to recognize the reality of providing services in a union environment. The result is not per se negative, but when a government reduces it waste-management workforce and sells its equipment, it may find itself at the mercy of contractors who raise rates again and again. City leaders then are faced with the dilemma of accepting the escalating costs or undergoing the capital expenditure of restarting the jurisdiction's own waste-management services.

Technology

An organization's technology can range from standardized to un-programmed. The term may refer to hardware, as in the case of assembly-line production of automobiles and steel. In other instances, technology might be a term for one-on-one counseling in social service agencies. The goal of establishing a fixed technology is the standardization of the process to ensure identical output, whether it be machined parts or food and rent subsidies for the poor. The great leap forward of the industrial era came about as a result of standardization, as when Eli Whitney began the manufacture of rifles with interchangeable parts. Fine-tuning of machine calibration, moreover, has led to precision and a reduction in human error. Similarly, standardization of policies is thought to be central to the fair and equitable distribution of public services. Government simply cannot work if eligibility standards vary among welfare recipients. Likewise, standardization of bidding requirements for government contracts is an essential barrier to corruption.

Hyper-standardization, however, especially when it is nonessential, can lead to worker boredom, dissatisfaction, and alienation. Fast food restaurants are an excellent example of the cons as well as the pros of standardization. Virtually every bun has an equivalent number of sesame seeds, meat patties weigh the same, and the shape of the scooper and the size of the container guarantee an equal distribution of french fries to customers. No one's sandwich is any better or any worse than anyone else's. Cashier's actions are standardized by buttons on the cash register that allow the cashier to punch in an item rather than its price. Then, by punching in the size of the bill offered by the customer, the machine will calculate the difference between the bill and the amount owed and report on the change due. Standardization of the process has reduced the human element to tasks that have not yet been formulated for execution by machines. The result is dehumanization of the work environment and a total discouraging of worker initiative or creativity.

The various factors that influence organizational structure also can interact with one another. The U.S. Postal Service is an excellent example of the interplay of mission, environment, and technology. Granted a monopoly on first class letter delivery, the postal service therefore provided for the written information exchange that supported commerce and government as well as personal communications for nearly two centuries. Challenges from competitors with a technological alternative began with the telegraph, and then proceeded to the telephone. More recently, the revised and privatized postal service is threatened by overnight package delivery services as well as electronic letters and fund transfers that have further threatened the viability of the postal service's stated mission. Thus, the traditional bureaucracy with a fixed mission has adapted its own technologies and delivery modes.

Similarly, in the face of increasing costs, colleges and universities are exploring delivery modalities that differ from the traditional lecture/note-taking approach. Adaptation advocates are quick to point out that the lecture system is a carryover from medieval times when access to information was limited by the number of available books. Thus, a single person was made responsible for collecting the wisdom and passing it on. When the printing press made books widely available, the essentialness of lectures was decreased. With the advent of the information age, moreover, students in remote regions of the world will eventually have access to the collective wisdom of the world's most prestigious library collections through the Internet. The value of the lecture system is thus reduced dramatically, and financially hard-pressed administrators continue to seek new and cheaper delivery systems.

One of the most common alternatives is the self-paced class, which involves interactive computer programs that impart fact-based materials. Likewise, interactive media facilitates distance learning as well as enabling student groups to meet and interact without assembling in a single location. Those who oppose the change point to the dynamics of interpersonal communications among students and between teachers and students. Thus, a university president who wished to adopt technologically based modalities would be faced with altering core values that have been in place for more than a millennium.

Organizational Culture

> " *He will win whose army is animated by the same spirit throughout all its ranks.*
>
> *You will not succeed unless your men have tenacity and unity of purpose, and above all, a spirit of sympathetic cooperation. (Sun Tzu, 1988)* "

Organizations evolve consistent patterns of interaction over time. These reflect the values and operating styles of those running the organization. Continuing the university example, the senior faculties composed of teacher-scholars may be expected to oppose any attempt to alter the lecture tradition. Their greatest resistance, however, is to organization models that advocate the use of part-time faculty on an ad hoc basis because it diminishes the sense of university community, dilutes the capacity for collegial interaction, and centralizes authority in the university—thus reducing department and program autonomy. In addition, part-time faculties employed full time elsewhere cannot be expected to engage in systematic research agendas to advance the store of human knowledge that is the second critical mission of the university. This is a core belief among academics who reason that the current university would not exist were it not for the accumulated wisdom of past researchers that has been catalogued into the library system and codified into disciplinary specializations.

In organizations that lack the collegial spirit of universities, it is often difficult if not impossible to quickly make the shift to a participatory consultative culture after decades of hierarchy and unilateral pronouncements from above. The roots of this problem are twofold. First, humans fall into routines that are difficult to change. Second, over time, people tend to adapt to the organizational culture and internalize its values or they move on to another organization they can believe in. As a consequence, an incoming leader with a preference for consultation and power sharing may find herself faced with subordinates who do not wish to consult. Indeed, some of them may have been attracted to the organization because its structure and rules were well-suited to their personalities. Others may have had the initiative beaten out of them over time. The latter has the added danger of being contagious because cynicism is easily transmitted from employee to employee rather like the common cold.

Socialization of new members is critical to imparting the values that underlie the culture of the organization. Prime examples of this are the armed forces, which never take value socialization for granted. Officers, whether products of ROTC programs or the military academies, undergo four years of socialization to learn military values as well as leadership skills, military tactics, and doctrine. At the bottom of the hierarchy, raw recruits are turned into soldiers in a relatively short time. The purpose of "boot camp" is as much a matter of values socialization as it is of physical conditioning, marching in unison, and basic weapons training.

Few civilian organizations are willing to spend the time and energy on socialization found in even the most relaxed military organizations, nor should they. Nevertheless, too many organizations ignore socialization altogether or leave it to chance.

The reality of most organizations is that cultural socialization occurs on the job and is conducted by the first line supervisor and coworkers.

Meeting Mrs. Hendershot

There once was a county hospital in southern California. Then as now, the need for health care for indigent people was great and resources were limited. The emergency room of the hospital was staffed to service 6,500 patients per month. Unfortunately, its clientele were not aware of this limitation and so came to the hospital for ailments large and small in monthly numbers that ranged between 10,000 and 12,000. Patients came in cars, ambulances, and by bus; but the daily ritual was always the same—too few staff members growing more impatient with each passing hour of their shift as the line of those seeking service never seemed to diminish. The day shift supervisor in charge of this mess was a 50-something nurse named Mrs. Hendershot.

Hendershot was once described by a ward clerk to a new doctor who was looking for her for the first time as follows: "Look for a middle aged woman in a lab coat with blood stains on it and a stethoscope protruding from one pocket. She'll have on worn-out tennis shoes and a crooked nursing cap and her slip will probably be showing. She also walks on her ankles." When another nurse who had overheard the clerk's description chided him for his disrespect, the clerk replied, "Oh yeah, well 5 bucks says he finds her in the next two minutes."

The day shift crew under Mrs. Hendershot's authority assembled daily in the cafeteria for coffee before the shift started. This is where managers from the nursing office would bring newly recruited nurses to introduce them to the group and to place them in Hendershot's charge to learn both hospital protocols and emergency room operating procedures. These new nurses were often brand new graduates identifiable by the starched uniforms, polished shoes, white nylons, and a school pin identifying them as a graduate of this or that nursing school.

Enter Mrs. Hendershot, ankles dragging, a cigarette dangling from her lips and her hair already falling from under her cap. "Where's the new nurse?" she'd bellow. Upon seeing a new graduate she would exclaim. "Ah, not another baby! Well, come on honey I'll show you the ropes." With the new nurse hurrying along in her wake, Hendershot would shuffle off to the emergency room. At times like this, she could be heard to exclaim, "This place sucks boulders!"

Turnover in a high-demand profession like nursing is to be expected in a less than ideal working environment. Many of Hendershot's charges would leave for calmer environs in private hospitals or they would quickly transfer to ward duty. New nurses capable of coping with the stresses of the emergency room, however, would reveal themselves within two weeks to a month. They were often found before their shift in the cafeteria wearing a stained lab coat, smoking a cigarette and muttering, "This place sucks boulders!"

One can only wonder at the speed of the transformation. Here were these young people so dedicated to helping others that they spent four years in training, at their own expense, learning the values as well as the skills of their profession. Under Hendershot's tutelage, four years of professional socialization could be undone in a matter of a few weeks of reality therapy. The lesson for managers is to be careful who is assigned to orientate new recruits to the organization because they will inculcate them with their own values as well as teach them where the medications are kept.

The wise leader will move slowly when faced with an organization of well-meaning employees who are burnt out by overwork or who have endured years of managerial promises of improved conditions only to find that they are again being asked to sacrifice for the organization in hopes of a better tomorrow that never comes. So what is a manager to do?

A sagacious organization consultant warns his audiences that no matter how enlightened or participatory they are personally, a fresh face is not by definition a fresh start. When new managers assume their positions, they occupy a haunted space. They should know that there is a ghost living in their desk. It is the memory of his or her predecessor, who for a time will color the thinking of subordinates about their new leader. This can be particularly frustrating for incoming managers with a preference for a collegial consultative style who succeed an authoritarian manager. Overcoming the expectations left by the predecessor is a slow process that requires a tolerance for worker reluctance to take the initiative. And, the manager must be willing to tolerate errors on the part of subordinates as they take their first few tentative steps toward making decisions on their own. If a manager's frustration threshold is low, he or she should not assume a participatory approach to problems. Workers who are chastised for errors made while taking the initiative are not likely to risk a second attempt.

There are no quantum leaps in organizational change. Change-oriented managers are well advised to heed this maxim. Upon entering at the top of the hierarchy of an authority-oriented organization, the leader should guide by example, patiently seek consultation, and positively reinforce efforts at creativity and initiative no matter how banal. It is only through trial and error and reinforced incremental successes that strong collegial organizations are brought about.

At the middle and lower echelons of authority, developing collegiality is made more difficult if those above do not share a positive view of worker potential for motivation, competence, and initiative. Here one must tread lightly; nevertheless, it is possible to be open to suggestions, to be sympathetic to subordinates, and to encourage initiative regardless of the overhead support one receives for these activities.

Once workers begin to trust that their ideas are welcome, the participatory manager must be careful not to quash initiative. When a worker makes a suggestion that is impractical or that may have consequences that the worker did not anticipate, he or she should be told so in a sympathetic way. By thanking them for their suggestion and explaining why the manager is unwilling or unable to put it into operation at this time, a leader reinforces rather than frustrates the suggestion process. Failure to validate initiative will discourage further participation.

Animating rank-and-file members of an organization with a common spirit is, ironically, often more readily achieved in the public sector than in for-profit organizations. Despite their red tape, rules, and procedures, public service agencies possess an advantage not shared by profit-oriented private enterprises. Organizations such as police and fire departments, schools, and social service agencies employ people who sought out their positions for reasons beyond personal gain. Much the same is true of health care organizations. In these instances a leader can begin consensus building around agency goals that are shared by the rank and file.

For example, a large city's police department might find itself simultaneously undergoing budget cuts and union strife due to the threat of layoffs. The leadership would find it easier to convince rank-and-file workers to participate in training in the latest methods of community policing than to convince them that management and the union are singing from the same page of the hymnal or that there should be no anxiety about losing their jobs.

Begin by finding the common ground. Creating task forces to assess current policing needs in the community, the current distribution of patrol resources, and the design of training programs could be a great first step in bringing the workers together. People will not begin cooperating until they begin communicating. Working successfully on practical consensus problems forms the foundation for handling more contentious changes involving union cooperation in planning for layoffs. Bringing union leaders into the cutback discussion and laying open the books has at times enlisted union assistance in convincing very senior officers to take retirement to preserve the jobs of less senior personnel. Focusing on concrete issues has the additional benefit of co-identification with the rank and file.

Unlike executives in the private sector who may be recruited from organizations with very different missions, most fire and police chiefs, school principals, and directors of nursing began in the trenches. If rank-and-file members of the organization view the manager as one who moved *up* rather than just moved *in*, they will be more willing to cooperate in leadership initiatives. When appointed from outside the organization, managers who aspire to be leaders should begin by convincing the troops that he or she is one of them.

Workers in for-profit enterprises can also be motivated around consensus goals even though they may have been attracted to their current employment for a paycheck rather than a higher purpose. (For example, it is difficult to imagine someone dreaming of growing up to market sugar-coated breakfast cereals or to install lug nuts on automobiles.) Nevertheless, the overwhelming majority of workers come into the work place willing to exchange an honest day's work for a fair day's pay. They also have an inherent preference for doing a job they can be proud of rather than merely getting by. A number of organizations in both the United States and Japan have had great success by involving rank-and-file workers in Quality Circles (Berger, 1986; Deming, 2000). This approach does not ask workers to redefine the destiny of the organization or to choose one product line over another. Instead, they are asked how the products that they produce can be made better or their job assignments made safer. When their suggestions are welcomed and implemented, workers become personally invested in the organization and its success.

Summary

The foregoing considerations are critical factors in organizational success. Of equal importance is how well the leader understands the problems and develops viable solutions for them. Good ideas, moreover, will not work if the leader is unable to sell his or her vision and convince others to follow. In the words of Franklin Roosevelt: "The worst thing that can happen to a leader is to look back and see that nobody is following." In a very real sense, leaders must sell themselves as well as their ideas.

To summarize, hierarchies are the principal method for organizing large-scale enterprises due to their pure size and the need for coordinated activities across functional units. We know also that leaders need not be bound by hierarchy when innovation and adaptations are required. Nor must leaders be bound by the less than desirable punitive disciplinary systems that often characterized traditional hierarchies. Furthermore, no matter how rigid the control system, organizations fare best when rank-and-file workers and management are animated by a common set of values.

There is perhaps no better example of forming a consensus culture than the decision by David Ben-Gurion and other leaders of the infant state of Israel to resurrect Hebrew as the language of the new state even though it was not used regularly by anybody other than rabbinic scholars. This was indeed a visionary decision because the new state experienced an influx of Jewish immigrants from the world over who generally spoke only the language of the country from which they emigrated. But, by insisting that everyone learn Hebrew, the leadership of the new state bound the disparate groups together with a common language as well as religion (Ben-Gurion, 1963).

In the final analysis, structural considerations of the organization and the values that drive its operations are critical factors in deciding how to lead. Ultimately, one is limited by one's own personality and worldview. Leaders who are naturally gregarious and who are confident in their own abilities will engage others with ease. They tend to seek maximum input from a variety of sources and worry little about hierarchy and status of the source when considering the value of information. Such were the decision styles of presidents Franklin Roosevelt, John Kennedy, and Bill Clinton. On the other hand, the insecure leader will seek to maintain distance from the rank and file of the organization by developing reporting systems to limit their contact with subordinates and to filter their decision input through trusted aides. They often will seek to structure the information flow such that information they do not wish to hear is blocked, a la Richard Nixon. His bunker mentality in dealing with the Watergate affair led to tragic consequences for his administration. Such was also the case with Lyndon Johnson in the closing days of his administration, when the war in Vietnam pushed everything else off the presidential agenda and people with contrarian views resigned in frustration.

Looking past one's own preconceived notions to see the organization, its environment, and problems as they *are* rather than how one might wish them to be is a test of leader wisdom. Figuring out how to move the organization from where it is to where one would have it be, is the test of leadership skill, vision, and purposefulness.

4

Decisiveness

❝ *Always take all the time to reflect that circumstances permit, but when the time for action has come, stop thinking. (Andrew Jackson, quoted in Meacham, 2008, p. 262)*

Measure twice cut once. (H. Ross Perot, 1992 Presidential Debate)

Chi Wen Tzu always thought three times before taking action. When the master was told of this, he commented: 'Twice is quite enough.' (Confucius, 1979, p. 79) ❞

The above quotations exemplify the conventional wisdom on prudent decision making. They point up the necessity to carefully weigh alternatives rather than make snap judgments. And while prudence is encouraged, decisiveness is mandatory. What is not clear from the above is what information should underlie the decision. Furthermore, information gathering and decision latitude vary greatly at various levels of the organization. At progressively higher levels, decisions become more complex, along with the range of factors upon which they must be based. At the very highest level, decision making is a matter of creating a vision for the future of the organization, designing systems for obtaining this future, and coordinating the efforts of those at lower echelons who are responsible for implementing the systems. We begin at the base.

On the Front Line

Leadership at the base of the organization is frequently a matter of solving mundane problems on an ad hoc basis. The frontline supervisor normally is given responsibility for the productivity of a work unit as well as the work performance of individuals. Decision making entails implementing organizational policy according to a standardized set of rules. The supervisor is then expected to solve problems as they arise using common sense born of his or her personal experience. It should be noted that rarely do situations arise that are unprecedented or that put the organization at risk.

Experienced frontline managers seem to be able to keep their units humming along almost effortlessly. Less experienced supervisors often wonder how smooth operations are even possible given that each new day arrives with a fresh set of problems. Faced with decisions that are unfamiliar, the prudent supervisor can apply the general decision rules to good effect by measuring twice then cutting once. This means assess the problem, check to make sure that nothing has been overlooked, and make a decision. Unfortunately, brand-new supervisors are often given too little preparation. Two distinctive classes of error emerge in this situation.

1. The natural tendency to avoid error can lead to indecision.
2. Alternatively, the supervisor may make a quick, erroneous decision in order not to seem indecisive in front of subordinates.

In the first instance, not deciding may allow problems to fester and undermine the efficiency and morale of the unit. Subordinates who bring problems to supervisors do not want to hear, "I'll have to get back to you about that." When they hear this, subordinates often assume that they will never hear back. Indecision has been recognized as a weakness in leaders since time immemorial.

> " Vacillation and fussiness are the surest means of sapping the confidence of an Army. (Sun Tzu, 1988, p. 49) "

Vacillation on the part of the inexperienced is understandable. In the first instance, they may lack the experience to appreciate the problems that are brought to them, frequently by more experienced subordinates. Fear of making mistakes that will greatly affect the efficiency of the unit is a second possibility. In these instances, some will carry the problem to their superiors for resolution, which can diminish them in the eyes of the superior. Conversely, some will fuss over a problem, torn between not knowing how to proceed and fear of seeming foolish to their own superiors. The result can be what the French call *immobilisme*. That is, fear of moving on a problem may outweigh its threat in the mind of the manager, with the result that nothing is done until the problem becomes a crisis.

Those who are too quick to decide or who make gut-level decisions based on their emotional response to circumstances are as much at risk as the indecisive.

<blockquote>
❝ . . . those who are quick to anger can be shamed; those who are puritanical can be disgraced; those who love people can be troubled. (Sun-Tzu, 1988, p. 65) ❞
</blockquote>

A propensity to take every problem personally and to respond with anger when simple direction is needed discourages subordinates from reporting problems from simple fear of their superior's response. Furthermore, personal slights and attacks on character, while they may bring about immediate ostensible compliance, are in the long run often destructive to interpersonal relationships and detrimental to organization aims. Those who are overly confident in the righteousness of their motives and who hold everyone to a strict code of conduct beyond what is necessary to maintain good order and discipline, can find themselves without friends when they personally make mistakes. Finally, managers who are fearful of hurting someone's feelings or incurring the resentment of workers for requesting greater effort may find themselves manipulated by subordinates. Or they may duck hard decisions for fear of causing controversy. They often perform work themselves that should be delegated to subordinates.

Walking the middle ground is the preferred choice. Finding the middle, however, often proves challenging. What new managers would do well to learn is that on the front line of the organization, a decision choice rarely solves a problem permanently. Conversely, bad choices rarely have consequences beyond the unit, as many a dissatisfied subordinate can testify. That is, the work unit may suffer as the result of poor choices that the upper-level bosses never hear about. Armed with this knowledge, the frontline supervisor can make decisions within his or her discretion without fear of a career-ending mistake.

So how is one to proceed using this decisive framework? First, few people bring up problems for which they have not already devised a preferred solution. The leader might therefore proceed by asking the subordinate to detail the problem as he or she sees it. The supervisor might then challenge the subordinate by asking for at least two potential solutions to the problem. Second, one should examine alternatives for their potential as a solution to the problem at hand. And one should ask subordinates to assess any potential pitfalls or negative consequences of the alternatives. Proceeding thusly, most mundane problems can be solved. A wise manager once said, "It's not like what's being suggested has not been tried before. And, wrong decisions are not likely to have long-term consequences." Just to be safe, however, one can authorize the subordinate to implement the preferred decision, then set a date for the subordinate to report back on the impact of the choice. If the problem is solved, great. If not, the manager can then look more deeply into the situation or try an alternative response (Etzioni, 1967). If this too fails, one is very likely either attempting to solve the wrong problem or is merely treating a symptom of a larger problem that requires closer examination or consultation with superiors.

When approaching a superior, one should be prepared to brief him or her on the nature of the problem and to report on the actions that one has taken to date. Subordinates who have taken the initiative to act within the purview of their authority but who recognize that they need help and advice demonstrate both self-confidence and discretion, which are valued traits for those wishing to get ahead. An air force colonel once offered this case in point:

Trouble in the Tower

A young officer called me from the control tower at 2 AM to report that an air cargo plane was experiencing mechanical problems and was getting low on fuel. The officer reported that he had given the plane authorization to land immediately, notified emergency services, and that he was diverting other incoming planes to alternative bases. My response was to keep me posted. On the other hand, had the officer in the tower reported a plane in trouble and wanted to know how to proceed, I would have told him to the take the above steps and that I would be there in five minutes.

Problems that contain interpersonal elements or that pertain to work distribution or the interface between work units must be approached with caution. The leader must take pains to examine all sides of the issue. The Marquis of Pombal ruled the Portuguese empire in the stead of a very weak king from 1750 to 1777. The following tidbits of wisdom are abstracted from a letter from the Marquis to his brother as the latter prepared to assume his duties as governor of Brazil:

> *Learn how to disguise and forget your own personal injuries.*
>
> *Alter nothing by force or violence but use careful discretion in correcting inveterate customs even though they be shocking. He who gives vent to his passions is a slave of them and undermines his own authority.*
>
> *As nature gave you two ears, one should be for the accuser and the other for the absent defender. (Marquis de Pombal, 1966, pp. 132–136)*

As noted in chapter 1, presenting a confident "command presence" is vital to those who wish to lead others. Pombal also shared the view of modern sages of organizational change that change is best achieved by developing consensus around a new set of values. Pombal, like Sun Tzu, always recommended against becoming a slave to one's passions because they sap one's judgment, which can lead to devastating errors.

Of particular note in Pombal's priorities was his concern for weighing evidence by hearing both sides of an issue before acting. Of course, not every subordinate who carries tales is seeking to advance his or her career at the expense of a colleague. Conversely, one should not assume that everyone who reports a problem is acting out of selfless concern for the betterment of the organization.

The Chair's Dilemma

The newly elected chair of an academic department was approached by the department's newest hire, who proposed a change in department policy to prohibit faculty members from using their own textbooks in the courses they taught or to otherwise advance their personal interests through their classes. When asked why he cared so strongly, the junior faculty member stated that it was a matter of professional ethics. He offered the example of his own dissertation advisor, who refused to use his own books in his classes even though he was a renowned expert on the topic.

The chair recognized that such a change in policy would pose a problem in the department because several senior professors, including the chair, used their own books in their classes. A further complication was the adoption of textbooks by colleagues. Thinking that he might have hit upon the real problem, the chair asked if the young professor was feeling pressure from senior colleagues to use their books in his classes, which in the chair's mind would constitute a breach of ethics. The young man responded that he was feeling no such pressure but that using a colleague's book would not pose a problem. The chair said he would look into the matter and schedule it for consideration by the department.

A consultation with a senior member of the faculty regarding university policy revealed that there was no such prohibition in any department on campus. The colleague further suggested that such a change might require a vote of the faculty senate because it would alter the definition of academic freedom as currently practiced at this university.

A conversation with another colleague who kept his finger on the pulse of the department revealed that a very senior member of the department routinely granted individual studies credit to the students who conducted exit interviews at polling places during elections. The practice resulted in students being given a semester's credit for one day's work, which did not meet university standards for the amount of work necessary to receive independent study credit. Furthermore, the chair learned that the data was subsequently sold by the instructor to a local television station.

(continued)

When asked about the allegation, the giver of credits confirmed that he had done so in the past and planned to do so in the upcoming election. He indicated that if the practice was not acceptable he would cease granting credit even though he believed that students gained valuable practical experience from the exercise.

True to his word, the chair raised the subject the next day with the junior faculty member. To his surprise, the chair learned that the assistant professor was fully aware of what had transpired and was not disturbed when told that disallowing faculty to use their books would not be in accord with department and university norms and that changing the practice would require a department vote, which would probably result in an affirmation of the current practice. The chair offered to place the proposal on the agenda of the next department meeting if the junior colleague insisted. After stating his continuing opposition to the practice of using one's own book, the assistant professor agreed to drop the subject. When pressed by the chair as to why he raised the subject, the junior faculty member admitted that the perceived misuse of student labor and independent study credits was his real concern. The frustrated chair asked why the young man had not just come forward with his real and very legitimate complaint? He then confessed that he did not wish to appear to be "ratting on a colleague." Apparently he preferred to kill a fly with a shotgun than to raise the real issue directly. Fortunately, in this instance the chair used both his ears.

> **❝❝** *Where you stand depends on where you sit. (Miles' Law)* **❞❞**

What is often more challenging than problem solving is devising procedures to enhance productivity without sacrificing morale or program effectiveness. Achieving this requires a shift in perspective from that of an individual to a unit-wide view.

Supervisors are normally chosen because they have proven themselves to be good at tasks assigned to them at lower echelons. Few people are promoted because they are bad at their jobs. Unfortunately, promotions sometimes go to the most senior subordinate out of the need to fill a position quickly or in the mistaken belief that experience is additive. That is, 10 years in the position is five times as valuable as two years. In fact, 10 years may merely represent two years repeated five times.

Even assuming that the best and the brightest are promoted, the change of role is no less impactful. As a practicing professional, one strives to do a good job and searches for ways to more efficiently perform the work. Then, suddenly, and often with no prior warning, one becomes a supervisor. In this capacity one must make work assignments, organize subordinates, and monitor the flow of the work. One must also look to achieve ends that are common to all unit members such as improving customer relations, outreach to new clientele, cutting costs, and so forth.

At first blush, these tasks may appear obvious—they are not. This is especially true of professionals whose educational preparation was devoid of managerial training. Engineers, nurses, teachers, and social workers in particular share this deficit. The faculties of these various disciplines continue to emphasize technical preparation despite alumni reports that their job assignments involve team leadership and directing others almost from the first day.

While teaching a supervisory workshop for vocational rehabilitation managers, this author emphasized the difference between the role of professionals and their managers by dividing participants into groups and assigning them the task of devising a set of performance evaluation criteria for rehabilitation supervisors—with one caveat. They had to devise rating criteria that were not aggregates of the collective production figures of their subordinates. After an hour they still could not come up with anything. By their lights, their personal productivity was merely the sum of the unit production. We spent the rest of the session discussing motivation, management, innovation, leadership, and employee development.

The easiest trap for new supervisors is the temptation to do it themselves. Many supervisors fall prey to this because they're overwhelmed by the pressure to produce. For example, the supervisor of a national call center received her position due to her uncanny ability to close sales. Her promotion immediately put a dent in the productivity numbers of the unit, as did the resignation of another superior performer who thought he should have been granted the promotion. The first response of the new supervisor was to supplement unit members by taking calls herself. Fortunately, her mentor advised her that this was, at best, a stopgap solution. The real solution was to recruit good people and to devise training to impart the supervisor's sales skills to others in the unit.

Good managers should act like coaches rather than players. Baseball fans frequently see team managers take the ball from a floundering pitcher and hand it to his replacement. Such managers do not, however, begin pitching themselves; nor does a football coach take over from a struggling quarterback. To carry the sports analogy a bit further, very few coaches and managers at the professional level were outstanding athletes in their own right. They are, however, masters of the game as a team effort. They correct performance gaps through player development and recruitment and they devise coordinated strategies. A rebuilding season or two is a common practice, after which results are expected. Finally, as a practical matter, few people possess a multitasking gene sufficiently strong to participate directly in routine production activities while simultaneously overseeing the full scope of worker activities. (A notable exception was the basketball great Bill Russell, who could play center while acting simultaneously as the coach.)

Managing at the Middle Rung

Up an echelon from supervisors are middle managers whose responsibilities may involve coordination of several work units. They also have the additional task of managing resources. The middle manager perspective must balance day-to-day production with longer term organizational strategies. They must look not only at what is being done within the organization, but they also assess the organization environment for changes that might affect the unit and devise appropriate adaptations. For example, middle managers of municipal programs may be called upon to scale back the implementation of policy initiatives during budgetary slowdowns. Thus project managers in an airport authority may find it necessary to delay the completion of a new terminal and its access roads for a year or two until funding becomes available. Truly effective managers try to anticipate fluctuations in the organization's environment and make adaptations almost before they become necessary.

The middle manager often must oversee the activities of several work units that may have disparate missions. Ostensibly disparate work units often are subtly interdependent so that a malfunction in one unit impacts the other. Mid-level managers often find it necessary to point out unit interdependences that unit supervisors have failed to recognize. Returning to the call center example, a lack of trained staff in the call center impacted directly on the referrals to various company facilities that, in turn, impacted the profitability of the entire enterprise. The challenge for the manager who oversees the call center supervisor is to anticipate a problem and allocate sufficient resources to make necessary adaptations. The manager must also allow some time for the adaptations to take place.

Mid-level managers may also need to integrate the activities of various specialty units that are not strictly interdependent. It is not infrequent that leaders of the subunits view other units as competitors for scarce resources and regard supervisors of other units as the competition for promotions and authority. Thus, middle managers must also seek balance between strong egos who do not wish to report to others whom they dislike personally or who seek to gain power over their own work units, driven by ambition rather than organizational rationality. A division chief at a NASA facility once confided that he took the position so that he would not have to answer to a colleague whom he considered to be a jerk. He went on to confess that division matters often were placed on the back burner as he continued to dedicate the majority of his time to completing his own scientific projects—an extraordinary admission but a cautionary tale for those making the promotions.

Perhaps the most overlooked of the necessary tasks of the middle manager is the mentoring of subordinate supervisors, especially those who are newly appointed to their positions. Regular meetings in which subunit activities and problems are discussed are a good middle ground between the temptation to micromanage and the tendency to throw supervisors into the organization mix to sink or swim on their own. Care should be taken to ensure that the person does not feel micromanaged. For those with the time and talent, the Socratic method can produce marvelous results. Plato relates how Socrates taught not by the didactic laying down of principles and rules but by asking probing questions of his students such that they arrived at the answers through their own insights (Plato, 1901). Confucius advised teachers not to provide the answer until students had struggled to the limits of their ability to solve the problem themselves.

> *I never enlightened anyone who has not been driven to distraction by trying to understand the difficulty or who has not gotten into a frenzy trying to put his ideas into words. (Confucius, 1979, p. 86)*

These ancient masters understood the benefits of *active learning* rather than being told to memorize the right answer. It is also instructive to note that the Confucian approach also screened for merit.

> *When I have pointed out one corner of the square to anyone and he does not come back with the other three I will not point it out to him a second time. (Confucius, 1979, p. 86)*

For many managers, mentoring is just a term from a management textbook with little practical application to the world of work. As one old-salt manager put it: "Yeah sure, I'll mentor the kid. But, what does that mean?" It means letting subordinates try and fail and processing their actions after the fact for ways that might have yielded better results. If over time they do not demonstrate the ability to see the other three corners by virtue of their insights, then they probably are not capable of further advancement.

> *Nothing is more necessary in governing a state than foresight, since by its use one can easily prevent many evils which can be corrected only with great difficulty if allowed to transpire. (Richelieu, 1961, p. 80)*

Organization-Wide Leadership

Hierarchies are characterized by narrowness near the top. Everyone cannot obtain the highest command levels regardless of whether or not they possess the requisite personal attributes of leadership. Ascending to the top of the pyramid is also a function of events and opportunities that have little to do with individual skills. No place is this more evident than in the quest for national leadership. The 2008 slate of presidential aspirants of both parties contained a number of competent individuals vying for the opportunity to lead. Among the circumstances influencing the outcome were the realities of two wars and an economic downturn. The size of the field of candidates was increased by there being no incumbent president or vice president seeking the office.

Fortunately for would-be leaders, gaining and maintaining the leadership position in most organizations does not require competing for popular support and generally does not attract competitors with the varied resumes of presidential candidates. In most instances, making it to the top is a matter of succeeding at the lower echelons of the organization. It bears repeating that organizations promote and/or recruit for top leadership positions based on demonstrated success at lower echelons. Operating at or near the top of the hierarchy requires a shift from operational to strategic thinking. In well-established organizations, strategic thinking often means making decisions that balance where the organization is against where it wishes to be. This requires balancing internal and external factors.

First, organization executives deal far more with the external environment of the organization than they do with operations. In the private sector, executives must constantly keep tabs on trends in the market, actions by competitors, changes in the economy, and so forth. Private-sector leaders must also handle relations with financial institutions, such as securing financing from banks and attracting investors whether they be individuals, private equity groups, or stockholders of publicly traded organizations. Internally, financial matters are treated by setting bottom-line expectations that are then tracked on a monthly or sometimes quarterly basis. Executives are interested in subordinate managers gaining or maintaining market share, operating efficiently and profitably, and they are held accountable for good-faith efforts to achieve progress in the strategic direction of the organization. If they are not meeting their established objectives they must devise solutions for correcting problems. Top echelon executives may make suggestions but they simply do not have the time to intervene personally in every division of the organization.

Public sector executives too are preoccupied with external matters. City managers, fire chiefs, and so forth are constantly engaged at the point of interface between the organizations they lead and their environments. Finances are always an issue, such as getting a city council to support a temporary sales tax increase to fund construction of a new firehouse. Once the council has approved the plan, however, it may also be necessary to put the tax to a vote of the people. In places like California, a two-thirds vote is required to levy taxes. Thus, the fire chief, the city manager, the mayor, and the members of the council must combine their efforts to convince voters to tax themselves.

Public officials, whether elected or appointed, have a fiduciary responsibility to taxpayers to be prudent stewards of the public purse. They are also responsible for the prevention of fraud, waste, and abuse. Officials of Orange County, California, for example, allowed financial managers to take significant risks with public reserves by investing them in junk bonds. When the junk bond market went bust, so did the creditworthiness of the county. Fallout from the debacle fell upon elected and appointed officials alike (*Los Angeles Times*, 1998).

The ideal private and public sector managers can usefully be classified into two archetypes of leadership. One is the **rainmaker** who is driven by competition and the obtainment of profits—lots of profits. Leadership success is easily identified by the market share of the company, its profitability and share values, and dividends to investors. The **statesman** is an alternative archetype borrowed from Anthony Downs (1957). Statesmen are expected to expend resources wisely, let contracts to the lowest responsible bidders, and to ensure that government operations are transparent. While the mission of the rainmaker is to maximize profits, the mission of the statesman is to optimize services within the constraints of available resources. More important is the responsibility of the statesman to faithfully execute the policy directives of elected officials. When policy differences become irreconcilable, the statesman is expected to resign his or her position. Contrast this with the behavior of some rainmaking executives in the private sector who, when they find themselves at loggerheads with their boards of directors, contrive to usurp the position of the board chair—thus becoming the chair of the board as well as the chief executive officer.

> '*Tell me please which way to go,*' said Alice.
>
> '*That depends a great deal on where you wish to go,*' said the cat.
>
> '*I don't really much care where,*' said Alice.
>
> '*Then it really doesn't matter which way you go,*' said the cat. (*An exchange between Alice and the Cheshire Cat in* Alice in Wonderland, Walt Disney Pictures, 1951)

At the end of the day, organization-wide leadership involves choosing a direction and then making decisions around that choice. Whether they strive to be rainmakers or statesmen, executives are expected to exercise their best judgment in the interest of the organization. The rainmaker, for example, might wish to establish a software company to develop and market an application to fulfill a perceived need in the marketplace. The first step is to develop a business plan that defines what is to be done, in what time frame, and at what cost. The plan would also contain a projected start date and define the anticipated return on investment.

In the dot.com boom of the early 1990s, the above process was followed to launch startup companies, which developed a product and marketed it for a time before taking the company public. Going public involved retaining a major financial institution to handle the offering. These endorsements lend the investment house *bona fides* to the company. Then, on a specific date, shares are offered for public purchase. By following this model, Microsoft executives became multimillionaires in a single day. In the decades since, multiple entrepreneurs used the IPO (initial public offering) model to great success even after the dot.com bubble burst in the late 1990s. The efforts of many other would-be rainmakers ended in failure. Operating in this high-risk environment requires supreme self-confidence, an unwavering commitment to the company's goals, and an exaggerated risk tolerance beyond those found in the rest of the herd.

The rainmaking personality is highly suited to self-defining profit-driven enterprises. The rainmaker would be out of place in established institutional organizations whose operations are guided by the principle of prudent continuity of services to an established community. These latter traits are often antithetical to innovation. As noted by Peter Drucker (1969), companies that historically possessed every advantage for innovating frequently failed to capitalize on likely opportunities. In the 19th century, railroads dominated transportation systems and commanded huge resources, yet they did not invest in the automobile. Similarly, automobile manufacturers with their mastery of assembly-line production methods overlooked the opportunity to manufacture aircraft.

The 1990s saw the blockbuster book *Reinventing Government* (Osborne & Gaebler, 1993) challenge conventional wisdom on how government should be managed. There is much that can be improved in bureaucracies, whether public or private. However, allowing career officials to innovate, create, and reallocate without accountability is a formula for disaster and fraud. Reducing accountability is an invitation to corruption. Strict accountability in the public sector was created to protect the public interest from being sacrificed to private greed. The reinvention advocates argue that society has evolved beyond the corruption that marked an earlier period. The behavior of individuals and groups in the relatively unregulated financial markets in the current decade suggests that private greed cannot be left to individual self-regulation, much less the distribution of public funds.

Universal Leadership Expectations

Having discussed the differences in the role expectations between rainmakers and statesmen, the discussion now turns to the roles that transcend the stereotypes. Despite their apparent differences, there is considerable overlap between the roles of our two archetypes. There are times when rainmakers must be good stewards of organizational resources. Conversely, statesmen are expected to take appropriate risks for the benefit of the public. In addition there are expectations shared by both. These include accurately assessing the environment, making appropriate adaptations as problems arise, and balancing between short- and long-range organization goals. These overlaps are illustrated in Figure 4.1.

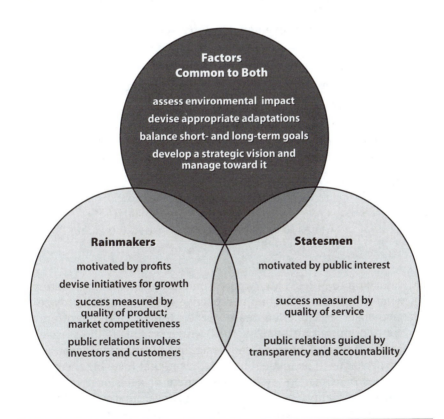

Figure 4.1   Interrelatedness of Leadership Expectations

> **❝** *Probity: adherence to the highest principles and ideals. (Merriam-Webster's, 2003)* **❞**

Reasoned Decision Making

The overriding expectation of both rainmakers and statesmen alike is that they exercise their best judgment in the interest of the organization. They should be temperate when necessary and bold when possible. They should act dispassionately and, above all, rationally. Rationality is the orderly application of decision theory at its most fundamental level. The steps are:

1. Define the goal or the problem to be solved as specifically as possible.

2. Examine alternative courses of action with regard to:

   a. their potential for achieving the end in question, and

   b. any secondary negative or positive impacts they may have on the organization.

3. Choose an alternative and develop a specific strategy for achieving it:

   a. give specific detailed instructions to subordinates and

   b. hold them responsible for achieving specific objectives.

4. Implement the strategy with scheduled benchmarks of progress and clear lines of accountability.

5. Evaluate the outcomes and impacts of the strategy and make appropriate adaptations (see Sylvia and Sylvia, 2004).

> **❝** *In this sphere of doing, it is generally said that the end we seek is not consistent studying or knowing the different things to be done; it consists in actually doing them. (Aristotle, 1998, p. 356)* **❞**

But, returning to Miles' Law (where you stand depends on where you sit), what is rational from one perspective may seem foolhardy to an objective observer. Nobel Laureate Herbert Simon therefore offers the concept of **bounded rationality** (1984). Such was his faith in reasoned decision making that he proposed designing organizations around the specific decisions to be made. Simon believed that focusing the reasoning abilities of managers on a limited range of decisions would optimize decision quality. He further noted, however, that what is rational varies with one's perspective. What is in the self-interest of individuals also varies. For example, a corporation might seek to finance a restructuring of corporate debt using the employees' pension fund. In exchange for their agreement to the plan, individuals would be given ownership shares in the company. Such strategies are often a final attempt to remain solvent in a hostile, competitive business environment. Young workers seeking to sustain their livelihood would see a yes vote as personally rational as well as in the long-term interest of the company. Those nearer to retirement, however, could be expected to vote no to preserve their fixed benefits.

Similarly, what is reasonable for the organization can differ significantly from what would seem universally rational. For example, in 1962 the administration of John F. Kennedy chose to impose a blockade on the island nation of Cuba to prevent the introduction of intermediate-range ballistic missiles belonging to the Soviet Union. The Kennedy administration believed that the deployment would give the Soviets an unacceptable strategic advantage because of the proximity of Cuba to the U.S. (90 miles.) It would no doubt neutralize the joint U.S.–Canadian early warning system deployed in the far north to identify an incoming Soviet attack with intercontinental missiles launched over the North Pole. Furthermore, the deployment would greatly strengthen the hand of Fidel Castro, whom the U.S. viewed as a threat to peace and security in the hemisphere as well as a fountain of support for revolutions against regimes throughout Latin America that were militarily and economically allied to the U.S.

The decision to use a blockade (dubbed a quarantine for public relations purposes) was arrived at through a series of decision iterations that ruled out a simple diplomatic protest at one extreme to air strikes at the other. Implementation began with placing the military on worldwide alert and lining up strategic support from critical European allies, especially the nuclear powers of England and France. The president then announced the quarantine on national television to enlist public support. The blockade was put in place and a simultaneous diplomatic initiative was undertaken at the United Nations to justify American actions and to line up world support to place pressure on the Soviets to forego their plans for missiles in Cuba. In a very few days, the "Cold War" was brought to the verge of a full-fledged nuclear conflict that would threaten the survival of humankind on earth.

The matter was ultimately resolved through an accord in which the Soviets agreed not to deploy more missiles in Cuba and to remove those that were already there. They further promised to never again deploy them in Cuba. In exchange, the U.S. pledged not to invade Cuba and to withdraw U.S. intermediate range ballistic missiles from Turkey; that is, from the southern border of the Soviet Union.

Rationally speaking, the Kennedy administration arrived at the determination to blockade Cuba through an orderly and reasoned assessment of alternatives to achieve the President's stated intent: "The United States cannot and will not accept the presence of Soviet missiles in Cuba" (Allison, 1999). From a perspective of objective rationality, however, the decision was less justifiable. A citizen of Fiji, for example, might find the risk of a nuclear holocaust unacceptable in order to secure America's perceived security interests.

The evidence suggests that Kennedy acted in part of out of his own profound sense of history and his personal place in it. No American president with the exception of Lincoln during the American Civil War had permitted a European power to establish itself in the hemisphere since the Monroe Doctrine of 1823. The record also suggests that Kennedy was angered by the behavior of Soviet Premiere Khrushchev, who had assured Kennedy at a summit early in 1962 of his wish to improve U.S.–Soviet relations (Schlesinger, 1965). Finally, historians have noted that the massive Soviet arms buildup in the last half of the 20th century stemmed directly from their perceived humiliation during the Cuban missile crisis.

The foregoing is not to suggest nefarious motives on the part of President Kennedy. Neither should we allow hindsight to inspire smugness in our review of the Kennedy decision. The point to be made is that rationality is bounded by time, circumstances, and the perceived self-interest of decision makers. Nevertheless, systematic decision making is preferable to snap judgments, especially when the organization itself would be threatened by a mistake.

Reason-based decision processes are best applied when decision makers take extra time in defining the problem ("measure twice and cut once"). Often, rethinking the problem leads to its redefinition. For example, hot-tempered outbursts in intergroup meetings may at first blush seem like a personality conflict between leaders. But, looking beyond the fact of their shouting and listening to what they are saying might reveal underlying problems such as work sequencing of shared assets or inadequate training of staff. Thus, a problem-solving retreat in which each is asked to express how he or she felt about the other's raised voice might be replaced with a problem-solving retreat that focused on work.

A second potential threat to executive decision making is the rush to implementation. Organizations can be so vexed by a problem that deciding on a solution is seen as the end, rather than the beginning, of the process. To the contrary, careful planning and implementation of the changes is as important as choosing to act. These tasks include choosing the method of implementation, then clearly and succinctly assigning responsibilities and putting in place a reporting system.

Changes are rarely self-implementing, especially those that require divergence from set routine. Organization consultants report frequent overlooking of this vital step in many organizations. The irony is that organizations have elaborate accountability systems to ensure faithful implementation of tasks that are substantially routine. Yet, these well-ordered systems assume that changes that are anything but routine will be understood by subordinates, calmly embraced by them, and implemented smoothly. To ensure that desired outcomes are achieved, executives should consider the following five factors in change management:

1. Take personal ownership of the desired change.

2. Assign specific tasks to specific individuals.

3. Designate a specific timetable for accomplishing the tasks.

4. Identify realistic milestones for reporting progress toward accomplishment. These may take the form of written reports, face-to-face briefing sessions, or both.

5. Make the achievement of the specified tasks a critical component in the appraisal/reward process of the organization.

Taking Ownership

Ownership means that organization leaders endorse the change as a priority at every opportunity. The leader raises the issue and expresses enthusiasm in the organization's newsletter and takes every opportunity to publically endorse the change at organization gatherings. The leader can also extend his or her presence into the various divisions where she or he engages in informal discussions with the rank and file to explain the change and why it is important. These sorts of meetings also allow the leader to convey commitment to change by reinforcing the message through emphatic speech, gestures, and body language.

Taking ownership also means backing the actions of those responsible for implementing the change when others challenge the direction being taken and/or the authority of the change leaders to make this or that decision. Regular progress reports to affected parties can reduce anxiety inherent in the change as well as enlist good faith adoption of the change by the program leaders; bearing in mind that rank-and-file workers will look to these leaders for cues on how to respond.

Designating Responsibility

Good faith intention to implement change can be undermined by the press of mundane tasks and the crush of minor adaptations that are necessary to routine operations. Change that is truly desired should be assigned to the most competent and respected individuals in the organization. These assignments should be made publicly and reinforced in private. Unfortunately, the most competent are normally already shouldering an inordinate share of the workload. Making the change a priority may therefore require some shifting of other responsibilities.

Specifying Timetables

Timetables should be devised in consultation with those responsi-ble for managing the various components of change. Executives can set goals and objectives and then ask the change leaders to provide them with detailed descriptions of what is to be accomplished and when by various work groups. This development of details can make good use of various software programs used in project management.[1] Reducing project components to deadline-specific attainment of objectives allows for fitting the change in with other program priorities and the efficient calculation of resource allocations.

Setting Milestones

This is an extension of the project calendar method. But by desig-nating specific reporting dates and scheduling progress meetings, the leader not so subtly reinforces the expectation that the project is a pri-ority. When asked to generate a written progress report and then publi-cally identify progress before their peers, change leaders tend to maintain the priority status of the proposed change.

Measuring and Rewarding Achievement

The maxim "that which is measured gets done" is truer when it comes to change management than when it is applied to routine opera-tions. The change is further reinforced when its achievement is rewarded. Remembering the Cardinal's admonishment to Louis XIII reported in chapter 2, ". . . there are few men who love virtue naked."

Some might ask how leadership of change differs from mere man-agement. Effective leadership in the change process

- displays ownership of the initiative,
- unequivocally sets expectations,
- demands accountability of results, and
- reinforces cooperation through recognition and rewards.

Final Thoughts

Real leadership is much more than merely weighing alternatives in an ordered fashion. Leadership probity describes decision making tem-pered by wisdom born of a synthesis of intelligence, experience, and temperament. True leadership is seeing what is beyond the ken of ordi-nary people and making adaptations accordingly. For example, when it appeared in the late 1990s that the dot.com bubble was deflating, pru-dent decision makers in the governments of the Silicon Valley began to

set aside a portion of their tax revenues in anticipation of the consequences of the downturn in technology stocks. These leaders understood that state revenues were heavily dependent upon capital gains
taxes. Thus, as the share value of dot.com companies declined, so too
would capital gains decline. When that happened, these leaders anticipated that the state legislature would cut the portion of state revenues
allocated to city and county governments. In other words, these forward thinking leaders "saw around the corner" and accurately predicted that state-level politicians would shift the decision to raise taxes
downward. By making prudent set-asides, these leaders forestalled the
full impact of the economic downturn on the services that they offered.

> " It does not take much strength to lift a hair. It does not
> take sharp eyes to see the sun and the moon. It does not
> take sharp ears to hear a thunderclap. What everyone
> knows is not called wisdom. (Sun Tzu, 1988, p. 27) "

Executives who lack vision tempered by probity are, at best, stewards
of the status quo.

Note

[1] Originally known as Gantt charts, these project calendars are available on the Internet.
The most versatile of these allow for tracking progress, fixing responsibilities, and calculating costs in materials, salaries, and so forth. They can be downloaded at
www.microsoft.com. Various free versions are also available on the Web. For examples
of how they can be used for change management, see Sylvia and Sylvia (2004).

Power and Communication

> *Power is the probability that one actor within a social relationship will be in a position to carry out his own will despite resistance, regardless of the basis on which the probability rests. (Max Weber, 1957, p. 152)*
>
> *Power is first of all a relationship and not merely an entity to be passed around like a baton or a hand grenade; that it involves the* intention of purpose *of power holder and power recipient; and hence it is* collective, *not merely the behavior of one person. (James MacGregor Burns, 1978, p. 13)*

Leadership communication is sometimes meant to inspire. More frequently it is meant to give direction or to solicit advice. The former is meant to tap into the emotions of the followers and to engender confidence in the leader. Very often it is meant to persuade the rank and file that what the leader wants from them is in their own self-interest. In this chapter we begin with some historical examples of the workings of power. We then turn to the business of persuading people to do what they might not otherwise do. The chapter concludes with some notes on formulating the message and clearly expressing the leader's intent.

Power Issues and Consensus

Leadership communications are most effective when they are based on mutual trust and commitment to a common set of goals. This is the case because power issues arise in the absence of consensus. In most instances, followers comply with orders because they agree with them. Or, at the very least, because they recognize that their leaders believe they are acting in the best interests of the organization. In these circumstances, followers act out of a **value consensus**; that is, they agree with the ends and recognize that any potential risks to the organization are necessary and acceptable. Followers also comply out of **value internalization**. That is, they obey because they recognize the leader's right to issue an order whether or not they agree with it (Sperlich, 1969).

Group thinking, or bringing the collective wisdom of the group together to identify problems and develop solutions, generally enhances rather than diminishes the process. Frequently, however, there is no time to build a consensus. One person therefore makes the decision. Military histories are filled with accounts of rank-and-file soldiers carrying out orders that they questioned—even at great personal risks—because they recognized the commander's responsibility for obtaining outcomes in the best interest of the organization. Trained soldiers also realize that noncompliance breaks down the entire command structure such that noncompliance with a lawful yet ill-conceived order can result in more damage than compliance.

Finally, people often cooperate because they are functionally interdependent with the order giver. That is, they simply cannot do their jobs other than through cooperative efforts with the leader. Suppose, for example, that the chief executive officer for a nationwide service organization decided to replace local marketing campaigns carried out through one-on-one contacts with a marketing and advertising campaign that was Internet-based. The new direction would be a major departure from the organization's traditional marketing efforts. Local managers might not agree with the strategy but would comply because their local operations are dependent upon attracting clients. So, if their preferred approach to building a clientele is no longer to be funded, their self-interest is best advanced by going along with the new approach.

The foregoing notwithstanding, change is normally uncomfortable and at times can prove downright threatening. It is incumbent on the leader, therefore, to give directions that are as precise as possible in order to minimize implementation problems. Furthermore, if leaders take the time to sell their vision they can achieve cooperation that is enthusiastic rather than merely compliant.

> *And it ought to be remembered that there is nothing more difficult to take in hand, more perilous to conduct, or more uncertain in its success, than to take the lead in the introduction of a new order of things. Because the innovator has for enemies all those who have done well under the old conditions, and lukewarm defenders in those who may do well under the new. (Machiavelli, 1992, p. 25)*

Getting What You Want

There are times when subordinates will not act as the leader wishes. At these times, the leader may have to engage in the use of power to persuade others to do what they otherwise would not. The remainder of this chapter addresses these factors.

Communications from leaders are not always meant to inspire. Most leadership communication is merely aimed at informing followers of the leader's wishes. Most situations require clarity and resolve rather than inspiration. The burden of communication clarity rests with the leader. The story of how Sun Tzu demonstrated his generalship for the emperor is instructive here. The sage began by asking the emperor to identify his two favorite concubines. The general then divided the remaining courtesans into two groups, placing a favorite in charge of each. Sun Tzu instructed the two leaders that he wanted the groups to practice marching for a while, then pass in review for the emperor to determine which of the groups had the best marchers. The first review resulted in chaotic lines and much giggling. Sun Tzu then took the two leaders aside and patiently repeated the instructions, taking unto himself responsibility for any lack of clarity in his first orders. After another period of practice the women again passed in review with the same chaotic results. This time, much to the chagrin of the emperor, Sun Tzu ordered the beheading of the two favorites. He then asked the emperor to identify his next two favorites. Sun Tzu repeated his instructions, time was given for practice, and a third review was undertaken. It is said that the courtesans marched with the precision of seasoned soldiers (Sun Tzu, 1988). The message to the emperor was that if placed in command of the army, Sun Tzu would use patience to clearly explain his intent; but would achieve compliance ruthlessly when necessary.

Obviously, the iron discipline of Sun Tzu would be inappropriate and punishable by law in modern society; nevertheless, precision of instruction and purposefulness in one's tone are essential to subordinate compliance. Orders that are imprecise or unclear are susceptible to interpretation by subordinates, who may disagree with the leader or treat the order as wishful thinking rather than a direct command.

Richard Neustadt (1991) wrote a primer on presidential leadership that specifies that the following circumstances must all be present for the presidential order to be obeyed without question.[1]

1. The president's position must be clear and unambiguous.

2. The person receiving the order must recognize the president's authority to give the order.

3. The person receiving the order must have the ability to carry it out.

4. The person receiving the order must perceive compliance as being in his or her best interest.

5. The order must be given publicly.

All Instructions Must Be Clear and Unambiguous

One should never give an instruction that ends with the phrase: "you know what I mean?" Managers cannot express their desires in ambiguous terms because it is too much to expect that subordinates will interpret vagueness correctly. Nor should one expect that a vaguely stated order will be interpreted as an executive priority. Of course, one cannot give absolutely precise instructions on every issue. Time constraints and the press of other matters simply will not allow it. For example, President Eisenhower, whose own writings were clear and precise, lamented the fact that sometimes he would ask a subordinate to draft a document for his signature but that the resulting order would not be precisely what the president wanted. Eisenhower regretted the necessity of signing a nearly correct order simply because there was no time to rewrite it (Eisenhower, 1963). Nevertheless, to maximize outcomes that are consistent with one's intent, one should cultivate the habit of giving clear and precise orders. While very few executives can plead the press of presidential responsibilities, there are times when the demands of other matters can override one's preference for clarity and directness.

Authority Must Be Recognized

Leaders must also be emphatic about their expectations so that subordinates do not circumvent the instruction willy-nilly. President Harry Truman, in hindsight, noted that his position on American involvement in Korea quickly transitioned from protecting South Korea from North Korean invaders, to liberating North Koreans from communist oppression by force, to the containment of communist expansion. He therefore shouldered much of the blame for what transpired between himself and the commander of United Nations forces in Korea, General Douglas MacArthur. General MacArthur publicly stated that the United Nations should invade mainland China using National Chinese troops from Taiwan. The general's assertion was absolutely contrary to the president's desire to contain the war to the Korean peninsula. Nevertheless, Truman was naturally reluctant to fire the hero of World War II's Pacific Theater. He did so in 1951 only after several attempts to get the general to keep his tactical pronouncements in line with administration policy. Removing a field commander in time of war is the most extreme step a president can take even though it is within his powers as commander in chief.[2] Truman recognized the action as a personal failure of himself as a leader.

The MacArthur incident is a clear example of the truth of Neustadt's second point regarding subordinates' recognition of the president's authority to issue an order. MacArthur may have entirely misread the president's intent. It is more likely that he was attempting to expand the war into open conflict with China by publicly forcing the president's hand. There had been more than a little speculation that MacArthur was contemplating a run for the presidency in 1952. Finally, MacArthur may have believed himself to be so important to the war effort as to be immune to the authority of a machine politician from Missouri. In this latter instance, the general was wrong (Manchester 1978; Truman, 1955).

Receivers of Orders Must Have the Ability to Carry Them Out

Giving an order that is beyond the abilities of the recipient is futile and can be disastrous. During the Korean War, General Chesty Puller came upon an artillery battery in full flight from an unseen enemy. Puller stopped the vehicles and inquired as to what they were running from. The officer in charge reported that the battery was being pursued by enemy infantry that was too close to employ the unit's guns. Perceiving that the young officer was clueless, Puller immediately assumed command and deployed the guns to fire at point-blank range. Under Puller's direction, the advancing infantry was enfiladed with close quarter fire. Had Puller merely given the order and left, the resulting massacre would have been reversed.

Orders Must Be Perceived as in Receiver's Self-Interest

The fourth component of Neustadt's model is that the receiver of orders must believe them to be in his or her self-interest. This criterion is most valid in the political context, where the receiver may have a political base not controlled by the president. As President Truman wryly noted, "Ike (Eisenhower) will come in here and say do this or that and expect it to be done" (Neustadt, 1991). Truman suspected that the political arena was far different from Eisenhower's experience as a military commander—an experience that Truman believed ill-prepared his successor for the rough and tumble of politics. The former general learned this lesson the hard way when he sought to persuade the governor of Arkansas, Orville Faubus, to comply with a federal court order mandating the immediate desegregation of Little Rock Central High School in 1957.

The governor refused to obey the order, insisting that proceeding with desegregation would be a threat to public safety. The governor demonstrated his resolve in the matter by ordering the Arkansas National Guard to circle the school and prevent the admission of the nine African American students.

To prevent violence, President Eisenhower sent for the governor, who flew to Rhode Island for a face-to-face meeting on board the presidential yacht. According to his notes on the meeting, the president made it clear that he fully intended to carry out the court order, by force if necessary. Eisenhower reports that Faubus understood his position and agreed to allow the desegregation to go forward. In a news conference after the meeting, the governor indicated that he and the president were in agreement. Upon returning to Arkansas, however, the governor continued to refuse to permit desegregation. Members of a white mob attacked African Americans in front of the high school while police and guardsmen stood by. The president then brought the full weight of the U.S. government to bear on the situation.

President Eisenhower signed an executive order federalizing the Arkansas National Guard, thus placing them under his authority rather than that of the State of Arkansas, and he ordered that they withdraw from Little Rock. To replace them the president dispatched elements of the 82nd and 101st Airborne Divisions to quell the violence and to ensure the peaceful admission of the nine African American students. What we see in this example is a governor who defied a presidential demand to obey the orders of a federal district court. Were Faubus to have done otherwise, however, would have been an act of political suicide. By defying the president, the governor was playing to his own political base. Though he lost this confrontation, the governor was elected to five more two-year terms as governor (Sylvia, 1995).

The Alternative

After trying and failing to persuade the University of Mississippi to desegregate without violence, President Kennedy resolved the matter by dispatching federal troops, who remained on the campus for a year. Not wishing to repeat this error a year later, the president applied Neustadt's approach brilliantly to secure the peaceful desegregation of the University of Alabama. Governor George Wallace had sworn to stand in the schoolhouse door to prevent the registration of the African American students. Like the governors of Mississippi and Arkansas before him, Wallace could not roll over for the federal government without losing his political base.

A compromise was negotiated in advance whereby Governor Wallace was allowed to express his "states' rights" defiance of the heavy hand of federalism on network television; after which, the Alabama State Troopers were federalized and the governor gave in "to preserve the rule of law." So the Kennedy administration achieved desegregation in Alabama without federal troops. It did so by assisting the governor in saving political face. The implied threat in the negotiations was the specter of thousands of federal troops descending on the University of Alabama like they had previously descended on Old Miss. Governor Wallace thus was able to comply without committing political suicide.

Orders Must Be Issued Publicly

For a presidential order to be carried out, it is best if it is issued publicly. Presidents who give their orders publicly put recipients on notice of presidential seriousness in the matter. Defiance of a publicly given order, especially if Neustadt's first four criteria are met, constitutes a direct challenge to legitimate authority, which rarely has a positive outcome for the defiant party.

Of note is the fact that Neustadt pointed to the firing of MacArthur and use of federal troops in Little Rock as examples of the failure of presidents to use their power effectively. For Neustadt, effective use of power is to place the receiver of an order in a position where compliance is comfortable and noncompliance is fraught with danger. Neustadt thus prescribes that the person giving the order *minimizes* the uncertainty of compliance while *maximizing* the uncertainty associated with refusal.

The Judicious Use of Power

In the workaday world of most organizations, the problems are much more mundane than questions of national defense policy or the enforcement of Supreme Court edicts. More to the point, the legitimacy of the order is not often questioned; nor do subordinates question the authority of the order giver. Lastly, the receivers of the order rarely have their own bases of power. To the contrary, subordinates, especially subordinate managers, are so dependent on their bosses that they are more likely to carry out an ill-conceived policy than risk the displeasure of their supervisors.

Despite these realities of modern organizations, the elements of Neustadt's model remain relevant: the content of the order must be clear and unambiguous; the receiver must acknowledge the authority of the leader, possess the capacity to perform the desired action, and see the action as being in his or her own self-interest. Publicly given orders also have much more weight than those issued in private. In most cases, refusing a publicly given order constitutes gross insubordination, which is a basis for discharge.

There are, of course, exceptions—as when the refusal to comply involves actions that are illegal, unethical, or dangerous. In these instances, one may have recourse to the courts on the grounds that the inappropriate order violated the terms of one's employment contract or organization policy. For example, an accountant who is ordered to "cook the books" (i.e., to hide costly decisions or cover up inappropriate allocations of funds) might point to the canons of ethical conduct of professional accounting organizations and/or statements in the organization's bylaws and codes of conduct that require the highest standards of professional conduct. Ethical or not, one risks continued employment by refusing direct orders. As a sagacious attorney once noted, "A lawsuit is a poor substitute for a paycheck."

A Fire Chief's Fall From Power

The fire department of a West Coast city was experiencing turmoil and turn-over after three successive years of budget cuts and the appointment of three interim fire chiefs following the retirement of a long-time chief. The department also was beset by racial turmoil over a perceived preference given to White fire-fighters, who made up the majority in the firefighters' union. Latinos and African Americans were well represented at the ranks of lieutenant and captain, but were almost nonexistent at the rank of battalion chief. To deal with the problems, the city manager and city council decided to recruit a chief from outside the department who could bring a fresh perspective and new leadership. They were particularly interested in finding a chief who could resolve the ethnic tensions in the department.

The recruitment effort produced an African American chief who had success-fully led a much smaller department. The new chief was appointed with instruc-tion from the city manager to deal directly with the union issues. It should be noted that under the charter of this city, the fire chief reports to and serves at the will and pleasure of the city manager.

The new chief had to deal with updating department equipment and reinvig-orating professionalism through training that had been minimized during the cost-cutting years. These issues would have faced any incoming chief.

Solving the racial issue was another matter. The chief instituted training ses-sions, taught by himself, to help prepare fire captains for the battalion chief pro-motional exam. The training was ostensibly available to anyone. In reality, it was attended almost exclusively by African American candidates for promotion. In the subsequent round of exams, Black candidates not only improved their scores, but actually surpassed all the White test-takers. This ignited a firestorm of controversy. The predominately White firefighters' union charged publicly that the chief had taught the actual contents of the test rather than merely prepara-tory materials. The union also filed a grievance seeking to set aside the exam and to promote individuals who remained on the old promotion list. The chief responded that the charges were baseless and his supporters accused the union of racism.

The city manager was thrust into the cross fire, which was extensively covered by local media. The charges and countercharges escalated to the point where the city manager was compelled to intervene. The manager counseled the chief, encouraging him to defuse the situation and to seek an accommodation with the union. The chief refused flatly to do so, insisting that he had been hired in part to enhance minority advancement in the department and that was exactly what he intended to do. He insisted that the manager back him in the contro-versy because he had done only what he had been hired to do.

Sensing that she was left with no options, the manager asked for the chief's res-ignation, which he refused to give. She then issued a written letter documenting the problems of leadership, their policy differences, and offering him the choice of resignation or discharge. The chief refused to resign and demanded a hearing before the city council. The council refused and voted to back the manager. The chief was discharged, but the racial problems of the department remained.

Returning to Neustadt's advice, it appears that the city manager did not make her intentions clear or that the fire chief misinterpreted what he was being asked to do. In either event, once the matter became public, the conclusions were foregone. The chief refused to compromise as a matter of principle. The manager could not give ground either. The matter proved to be a huge embarrassment to everyone involved and the racial tensions within the department continued. It should be noted that a subsequent lawsuit by the chief was settled out of court for an undisclosed amount.

The foregoing is precisely why Neustadt averred that presidents (read: executives) cannot simply issue orders and expect automatic compliance. What is necessary is the judicious use of power or, according to Neustadt, convincing others that what one wants is what they should also want. To this end, Neustadt says one must maximize the uncertainty of noncompliance while minimizing the uncertainty associated with compliance. Minimizing the uncertainty of compliance requires benefits to the subordinate and a clear statement of support for his or her compliance. Maximizing uncertainty involves the use of an implied threat. A presidential example of this is when the chief executive is asked whether the use of force is being contemplated; the president and other administration spokespersons repeat the same message: "All options remain on the table, unless country so and so does X, Y, and Z." Consequences are left intentionally vague while expectations are clearly stated, as are the benefits of compliance.

Thus the city manager in our example might have said to the chief, "I want you to apologize for your racially charged comments. I want you to make a joint statement with me indicating that an independent review of the test preparatory training materials will take place to assure everyone that nothing untoward took place in the sessions. Third, you will suspend implementation of the new promotion list pending the outcome of the review. I will issue a statement expressing my full confidence in your leadership and the city's commitment to achieving diversity while adhering to the highest principles of advancement on the basis of merit. I will also increase your training budget to pay for human relations training for all personnel. And finally, I will meet with the union leadership privately and reinforce our commitment to fairness and my firm intention to support your leadership of the department. If you refuse to do any of the above, your employment will be jeopardized." Of course, there is no guarantee that had the manager acted as suggested here that the outcome would have been any different. What we do know is that the fire chief was not presented with any options that did not reflect negatively on his leadership.

The importance of leadership communications cannot be overstated. The matter rests not only on the content of the message but also upon how it is formulated and delivered.

Formulating the Message

Effective communication between individuals and organizations involves much more than broadcasting a clear message in the manner of television and radio stations, which monitor their signals for power and clarity. There is no guarantee, however, that anyone is listening or watching. Of course, stations get a sense of their success through rating systems that poll audiences for their preferences in listening and viewing. Ultimately, if they cannot sustain a sufficient viewing or listening audience they cannot attract advertisers. No viewers/listeners, no sales; no sales, no advertising; no advertising, no television/radio station.

Communications between individuals are much less technically complex but are often complicated by the affect of the sender and the predispositions of the listener. The communications process goes as follows:

> **A** formulates a message.
> **A** chooses his or her message medium such as the telephone, letter or e-mail, or face-to-face communication.
> **A** sends the message to **B**.
> **B** receives the message.
> **B** decodes the message.
> **B** attempts to understand the message by checking it against stored information, such as **B**'s personal experience and **B**'s own best judgment.
> **B** formulates a response.
> **B** encodes the response.
> **B** selects the response medium.
> **B** sends a message to **A**.
> **A** receives the return message.
> **A** decodes the message.
> **A** interprets **B**'s response using **A**'s stored experiences.

The process is not complete, however, until **A** indicates receipt of the return message and expresses **A**'s assessment of **B**'s response. In interpersonal communications involving persuasion, **A**'s reaction should not only say "message received" but also acknowledge **B**'s understanding of the original message with an effective response, such as, "I am glad you agree with me regarding the urgency of this matter. Your past work has meant a lot to me and has contributed to our division's previous success." Such a response by **A** expresses esteem and seeks to enlist **B**'s help going forward.

The Censure Message

Telling someone that they are doing well is perhaps the easiest part of leadership communication. Telling someone that they are performing poorly and must change their behavior is far more difficult. Negative responses, especially from one's boss, are at the very least discomforting and may even prove traumatic to the subordinate, depending upon content of the message and its method of delivery. Loudly criticizing a subordinate in no uncertain terms during a staff meeting is particularly humiliating. The goal of critical messages should be to alter outcomes rather than to inflict injury.

The importance of outcomes. A critical component of an effective corrective message is to secure changes in the behavior of the listener. As obvious as this may seem, many a manager has taken the time to carefully script what he or she wished to say, only to have the meeting end in an angry or tearful resignation on the part of the listener. (Of course, if previous attempts to correct behavior have gone unheeded, the manager may wish for a resignation.) Nevertheless, there is no need to cause unnecessary pain nor is it necessary that working relationships end badly.

A minimalist message might say: "You are not doing well enough and I want to you to improve." This formulation might be minimally satisfactory for initiating a dialogue because it establishes that the topic is the listener's performance and the speaker's dissatisfaction and it expresses the speaker's expectation of change. It is certainly better than falling back on the catchall line, "The company made me do it." By delivering a critique then invoking company rules and policies as the underlying motivation, the speaker seeks to shelter him or herself from the listener's wrath. In the institutional formulation, the manager invokes the organizational "they" as the source of the dissatisfaction, e.g., "Company rules clearly state that you must meet the production standards." This is fine for those who merely wish to supervise. Those who would be leaders, however, must make the criticism a matter of their own professional judgment and strengthen the message with the force of their own personality.

The most effective message is the one that specifies concrete behavioral changes. The following is an example of an effective critique.

A Critique that Motivates

The manager, whom we shall call Bill, might begin the discussion with the subordinate, named John, as follows: "John, I am concerned that your sales numbers for the last two months are low. They are significantly below what I expect from a salesperson of your experience. What can you do to improve them?" The

(continued)

point of ending the critique with the query is to initiate a dialogue. It has the added advantage of making the listener responsible for finding a solution.

In a perfect world, John would acknowledge his shortfall and explain the steps he is taking to correct it. For example John might begin, "I have already scheduled sales calls with my customers who have either reduced or canceled their orders to determine what is going on and hopefully to reconnect with them on a personal level. I've also developed several new leads and have sent out informational packets to them. In one case, I have scheduled a lunch with a potential customer who, as it turns out, was the college roommate of a close personal friend, who has agreed to join us for lunch." An appropriate response from Bill would include a statement of encouragement and the scheduling of a follow-up meeting to report on the outcomes.

If the preceding was actually John's response, the meeting would probably not have been necessary in the first place. More realistically, John is apt to blame an economic downturn or the obsolescence of the company's product line. The economic downturn argument is easily addressed. The old adage, "the rain falls equally on both armies" is applicable here. First, the manager should already know the validity of the economic justification and adjust his expectations accordingly. Of course, there may be no economic justification at all based on overall company productivity or the sales performance of John's peers. Bill should resist the urge to play "gotcha" and should particularly avoid a judgmental response. An appropriate response would be, "You feel as though the economy is hurting sales?" This response shows John that Bill heard him and it sets the expectation that John elaborate on his concern. John might respond, "That's right; nobody is interested in spending money right now." Bill might then say, "And what specifically are you doing to improve your numbers in light of your judgment about the economy?" This brings the discussion back to John's performance and reasserts that it is his responsibility to correct the problem.

If John has no concrete ideas to improve his sales, Bill can take the initiative by offering some specific strategies. Bill may also assert specific improvements that he wants to see along with the date for a follow-up meeting. Bill might say, "I want you to do A, B, and C. We will meet on date X to check your progress. Like I said at the beginning John, I am confident that a salesperson with your skills can handle this."

The reader will notice that at no time did Bill question John's veracity or his inherent worth as a person. Personal abuse or other strong language are excellent tools for starting a conflict. If, on the other hand, one wishes a change of behavior, a more circumspect approach is appropriate. The time to impose consequences occurs later, if in the follow-up meeting Bill learns that John did not follow his suggestions or that John tried but was just incompetent.

Leaders should not begin a corrective action with the threat of serious consequences. On the other hand, continual unwillingness to take punitive actions in the face of nonperformance could compromise the effectiveness of the entire unit. This is so because a willingness on the part of Bill to accept nonperformance on the part of John could be interpreted as personal weakness on the part of Bill and be viewed by other unit members as a license to reduce their personal performances.

How Not to Proceed

James is a senior-level probation officer in a large county. Mary, his supervisor, earned her position through 10 years of hard work as a frontline probation officer. She has been in her current position for six months and during that time she received several unsettling phone calls from parents of probationers supervised by James. These calls allege that James used abusive language toward them and their children, that James calls and says he is coming over and then does not show up, and that he generally treats probationers as if they worked for him.

Two weeks ago she received a disturbing call from the clerk of courts, complaining that James had not completed necessary evaluation work on at least five separate occasions, thus holding up the process in juvenile court. The clerk expressed particular concern regarding the discontent of the judges in these cases.

Mary was also concerned with James's attendance. James was coming in late and leaving early and appeared to be abusing his sick leave. Despite 25 years of service with the county, James had only eight hours of sick leave on the books, which he accumulated in the last 30 days.

Mary has been so busy learning her new position that she has been reluctant to raise these various issues with James, but she must now do so because his annual performance evaluation is due. In checking the file, she learns that James's previous evaluations rated him fully satisfactory. Then and there, Mary decides that, as difficult as it would no doubt be, she must address these matters head-on. Mary sends James an e-mail that instructs him to come to her office at 10 AM on Friday for his annual review. She receives a return message saying he will be there. On the appointed day, Mary waits until 10:20 before looking for James, only to find that he has signed out to the courthouse for the entire day. On the following Monday, Mary phones James and tells him to be in her office at 3 PM. When James arrives ten minutes late, he says, "Sorry I'm late, I was stuck in cross town traffic." Mary decides not to inquire about the steaming cup of coffee in his hand from the shop around the corner.

Mary begins: "James, I have received several complaints from the parents of your probationers charging you with unprofessional conduct and abusive language."

James says nothing for a few moments while he stirs his coffee and stares out the window. "That is a load of crap!" he says.

"Are you denying that you verbally abused your clients?" Mary says.

"You're damn right I am. How long have we worked together? Who are you going to believe, me or that bunch of skells?"

"I would prefer that you not refer to our charges as a bunch of skells," Mary says.

"Well, have we learned to play office?" James sneers. "Clients, skells, or whatever you wanna call them, they are lying and you can't prove otherwise," James says.

Mary decides to move on because James is getting agitated and the tone of his voice is making her uneasy. "Well, there is another matter I want to discuss: your work attendance. It's true we do not have a time clock but I notice that you often come in late and leave early. Does that sound about right?" Mary says.

"Listen Mary, I'm here as much as the next guy. Often I stop off to see probationers on my way to work. As for leaving early sometimes, everybody else does

(continued)

it too, on occasion. I usually do it only on the days when I am forced to work during lunch. To my mind, it all evens out," James says.

"But how do you explain your absolute lack of sick leave on the books? And what's your explanation for being sick on Fridays and Mondays?" Mary asks, getting angrier by the minute.

"Look, I don't like complaining but I have a number of health issues. My back is especially fragile since I was wounded in the Vietnam War. But I guess you're not old enough to remember that," James says.

"Why Mondays and Fridays?" Mary persists.

"Well I have an ongoing appointment with a chiropractor for my back problems on Fridays. Besides, this place stresses me out so much that I have been on pain medication and I sometimes just need a mental health day," James protests.

"Let's talk about complaints from the clerk of courts regarding your slipshod case management and that you often miss court deadlines that cause hearings to be postponed," Mary says.

"You got me there; my caseload is so ridiculously high that nobody can give the individual cases the attention they need. Look, when I started this job I had an average caseload of 75 to 80 clients. It's now gone to 250. So excuse me if I get a little behind. Anyway are you planning to put any of this in writing? Because if you are, I want my union rep here and I mean right now."

"I haven't decided whether to write you up or not. I just thought we should address these issues before starting a formal process," Mary says.

"Well, if that's it, let me know when you make up your mind and want to put something in writing so I can bring the union rep with me the next time. Now if you'll excuse me, I have work to do." With that, James leaves the room.

Mary cannot imagine how she'd gone wrong. She had merely tried to address issues of legitimate concern about James's performance. She had expected him to be apologetic and to accept her criticism. Instead, she received a series of excuses and the threat of union action that left her at a loss as to how to proceed. Mary decides to set the matter aside and get some other work done and to make an appointment later in the week with the director of human resources to solicit advice on how to proceed.

Mary is an excellent example of someone who was placed in a position of authority because of her subject matter expertise but who lacks the tools she needs to manage others. Her experience as a working probation officer developed in her a habit of asking very direct questions and demanding clear answers. Of course, the consequence for the probationers who refused to cooperate was referral back to court and possible jail time. Jail is not an option in James's case. More to the point, his is a civil service position, which means any disciplinary action must be fair, balanced, and appropriate for the offense in question because the matter will be reviewed by external authorities. Furthermore, because James's previous evaluations had been satisfactory, Mary must therefore show reasonable cause before attempting to discipline James.

From our perspective as observers, the obvious question is how Mary might have proceeded differently. First, she should have called James into her office the first time she received a complaint regarding his treatment of clients and counseled him in the matter. She might have said, "James—I've received a phone call from the parents of one of your probationers alleging abusive behavior on your part. As your supervisor I feel compelled to give this matter my immediate attention. Abuse of clients and their families is inappropriate at any time and I for one will not tolerate it from the probation officers in my unit. Now, is there any validity to these charges?" If she had any doubts in the matter after asking James directly, she should schedule a meeting with the complainant. If complaints from others followed, she should undertake progressive discipline. This might include a formal written reprimand placed in James's file. A recurrence should result in a suspension (many government entities give supervisors the discretionary authority to suspend an employee for up to three days without being challenged by the union or reviewed by civil service officials). More extreme actions could be undertaken if performance does not improve; such activities include suspension, demotion in rank, and ultimately discharge (Sylvia & Meyer, 2001). An early, assertive critique of a subordinate's job performance in one area can spill over to self-correction in others. If not, the foundation is laid for more serious consequences.

Similarly, Mary should have immediately addressed the problems of James's work habits, especially his court liaison function. Unlike his clients, the district attorney and sitting judges are not so easily dismissed. The institutional interface between the juvenile court system and the probation department is critical to the functions of each. It is a prime example of what we discussed earlier under the rubric of functional interdependence. Overseeing relationships between her staff and external actors is central to Mary's responsibilities as a unit supervisor. Finally, if James has been abusing his sick leave, this too should have been addressed previously.

The annual performance evaluation is not the appropriate venue for the initial addressing of disciplinary problems. Instead, James should have entered the meeting knowing that he had previously been put on notice regarding the three areas of his conduct that were in need of correction. Mary could then have focused upon the actual ratings that she was giving James in the areas of work performance, communications, client relations, and so forth. The fact that she chose to raise disciplinary issues during the annual evaluation might have caused James to feel blindsided.

An annual evaluation is a summation of one's performance, previous criticisms, and the corrective behaviors that have been undertaken. Furthermore, evaluations are normally post hoc activities. They are summative rather than formative. Matters in need of correction should be raised as they occur. Moreover, setting clear expectations for changes in behavior, then following up on one's instructions as a matter of routine, can be an effective means to correct behavior. And it can greatly reduce the stress of the annual performance evaluation.

Had Mary addressed the problems early and directly, James might have corrected himself. The annual performance review would become an overall performance assessment, informed by the previous corrective action memos. Mary's annual assessment would then be comprehensive and documented in writing should it become necessary to take appealable adverse actions. Under most civil service rules, employees cannot appeal a performance appraisal until it results in an adverse action (lengthy suspension, demotion, or discharge).

From our second example, one gets the sense that James has stayed too long at the fair. He clearly no longer gets satisfaction from his work. One also gets the sense that Mary and James have been colleagues for some time. As such, she may have a personal investment in James as a friend. Based on that relationship, she might choose to counsel as well as critique.

A Better Approach

Assuming Mary had been addressing issues as they arose, she might begin the appraisal interview by inquiring how James was feeling. Then, if there had been no appreciable improvement in his performance, she could try easing James into retirement. This could be done by noting his lack of performance and her knowledge of him. "James, I am sorry to note that we are still getting complaints from your clients and the clerk of courts. I say I'm sorry because you used to be one of the best probation officers in the unit and I really respect the way you handled whatever came your way. Now, with all your health issues, perhaps it is time that you started putting yourself first. I mean really take care of yourself. Look, you have 25 years of service and certainly have reached the age when most people think about retiring. Have you looked at what your income would be if you retired outright? Well, I took the liberty of calculating it for you. If we allow for your social security income and the fact that you would no longer be paying into social security, retirement, and union dues, you are practically working for nothing. That is to say nothing about the cost of business clothes, commuting, and so forth.

"James, the last thing I want to do is force you to end your career on a sour note. I'd much rather give you a retirement party and a gold watch. You don't have to give me an answer this minute. Let's set this review aside for a few days while you think it over. Go talk to personnel and see if I'm not right. Let's meet again in three days, shall we?"

In a great many burnout cases, people hang on simply because they don't know what to do with themselves in retirement. Laying out the benefits of retirement (minimizing the uncertainty of compliance) while holding forth the prospect of an adverse action (maximizing the uncertainty of noncompliance) could help James realize that what Mary wants is in his own best interest as well.

Of course, there's no guarantee that as Mary proceeds with her counseling approach, James will react positively. Quite often even the best intended messages provoke fear in the listener and anger in the response. For example, James might explode: "Let me get this straight, are you telling me that I must either retire or get fired? In the first place, you haven't got the guts to fire me. In the second place, I have both the union and civil service system to protect my interests."

It is a common instinct to respond to anger by displaying one's own anger. We saw that Mary's preferred response to stressful situations was to change the subject. Instead, she should address James's anger directly. She might meet his gaze and firmly say, "James, it is not my intention to threaten you or to make you angry. As your friend and colleague, I would like to see you conclude this matter with dignity and respect. My intention is that this unit will operate with the highest possible level of professional standards, which you do not currently meet. Please take a few days to consider the pros and cons of retirement. If after that time you still do not wish to retire, I will, in fact, put these negative comments in writing and place them in your personnel file. At that point I will work out with you a specific set of behavioral changes along with a timetable for achieving them. Your failure to comply will result in further adverse actions against you."

The simple fact is that a great many people in the workplace are finished as far as their career is concerned. They no longer receive gratification from their work and they wish to get by with minimal performance. Supervisors cannot realistically hope to convert substandard performers into superior employees. They can and should, however, set the expectation that the person perform satisfactorily. Failure to hold employees to a reasonable performance standard is to shirk one's supervisory responsibilities and to set a negative example to other employees in the unit.

The Medium Is the Message

With these words, Marshall McLuhan (1962) pronounced the decline of the written word, which since the invention of the printing press had exponentially enhanced the dissemination of knowledge. McLuhan recognized that the advent of television would remake the transmission of knowledge. Previous generations of children had escaped into and learned from printed books. Now, television would supply information and an escape from the tedium of the printed word.

McLuhan reasoned that words on paper required only a passive audience for the writer's lecture. Although readers might be mesmerized by the fiction writer's use of written images and gift for storytelling, most often this was not the case with nonfiction educational materials. Written materials were essentially what McLuhan termed a "cold medium."

By contrast, McLuhan viewed early color television as a warm medium because the images were transmitted with a limited palette of colors. The viewer's brain actively converted images into the full spectrum of color that we take for granted in the image we are watching. McLuhan wondered at the impact of the new, dominant medium on society, especially on education.

It is perhaps a feat of wonder that first-grade teachers are able to teach the application of an alphabet that was learned by watching *Sesame Street*, with its light shows and music. Educators struggle to teach reading skills that require personal application of the skill outside the classroom. When we add computer games and portable music devices to the distraction of TV, challenges to traditional education are multiplied. At this point, the reader may be wondering what all this has to do with managerial communication? The answer is that how one chooses to communicate can be as meaningful as the content of the message for obtaining results.

In hindsight, we can see that the actual impact of these communication modalities upon the written word has been mixed. On one hand, these electronic wonders have diminished reading skills in the population. But, the world of business still relies greatly on written communications. Written communication affords as much clarity and precision of language as one cares to take the time to formulate. However, the popularity of e-mail for high-speed communication among organization members sometimes has the opposite effect, encouraging haste and brevity. E-mail is certainly quicker than summoning someone into an office for a face-to-face meeting. Secondly, e-mail documents that the communication has, in fact, occurred, at least that it has been checked. Just as the laws of physics hold that "for every action there is an equal and opposite reaction," the same is true of e-mail communications. Because messages flow both ways, a quick inquiry about a project's progress may yield a written response that is murky, incoherent, and raises more questions than it answers. This requires a follow-up e-mail and then a clarifying response, etc. Of course important matters can be followed up with a phone call. The speed with which e-mails can be transmitted is a great temptation for workers to inundate their peers and their bosses with trivial inquiries that they may very well have solved using their own judgment.

McLuhan's pronouncement of the decline of the written word failed to foresee the soul-sapping reality of coming to work to find hundreds of e-mails on the server that, at the very least, must be sorted through to find the important messages. A related annoyance is the expectation of the message sender that the reply will be immediate. As one motivational consultant said, "I come to my office and the little light on the phone is blinking. I turn on my computer only to learn from my in-box that I am already behind and I haven't even started yet."

Those concerned with documentation use e-mail to form a written history of what is being communicated. But documentation also can have an equal and opposite reaction. A written message from one division manager to another complaining of unresponsiveness or inefficiency in the receiver's unit will probably elicit a terse reply denying the accusation and/or raising questions about the motives and efficiency of workers in the original sender's division, which in turn demands a written response. The best way to avoid such a war is to not let it start in the first place. Robert Townsend (2007), the man who made Avis number two, recommends doing away with e-mail altogether. He contends that covering one's actions with paper leads to distrust and counterproductive communication. Townsend recommends that coworkers act as if they are working toward the same goals. When problems arise, one should visit the other party or phone them in the spirit of cooperation rather than complaint.

The language one uses and the formatting of the message can say a great deal about the author. How one begins a message conveys one's attitude toward the recipient. An e-mail to one's chief executive officer should not begin with *Bob*. How much longer does it take to write *Dear Mr. Jones*? The concluding salutation can be equally important. Signing off with *Sam* or just *S* is too minimalist to be polite. Adding *sincerely, cordially,* or *respectfully yours* when combined with the formal opening can go a long way toward "making your manners," as they say in the Midwest. There is no excuse in the 21st century, moreover, for electronic messages that contain grammatical and spelling errors. Checking for mistakes communicates one's thoroughness and attention to detail.

The Oral Communication Alternative

Oral messaging is the preferred method of communication for the socially adept. Personal interactions in which one looks the other in the eye can be far more productive than a dozen e-mails back and forth. Of course, the "face time" of busy executives is a precious asset, not to be squandered. That said, one's capacity to bring the force of one's personality to bear on a problem far outweighs the loss of time—especially in matters of critical concern. The same holds true of group discussions, where leaders can punctuate their priorities with gestures, looks, and voice modulation. Group meetings are also invaluable for stating orders publicly. Extreme criticism and censorship should always be delivered in private. Nevertheless, public instructions to a subordinate put the leader's intentions on record and put the recipient on notice as well.

Analyzing problems in a group format can bring the full weight of the organization's problem-solving skills to bear. This method should be used judiciously, however, because time spent in strategy sessions is time taken away from other priorities. One mid-level manager lamented the army's previous use of what it called "tiger teams" to deal with agency priorities. It seems that the executive in charge of the division had a great many priorities and a commensurate number of tiger teams. The result was that all middle managers found themselves running from one tiger team meeting to another. Regular production problems went unsolved and managers found it difficult to talk to members of their tiger team, who always seem to be meeting with another group.

The Importance of Being Oneself

It is important to remember that one size does not fit all or even most. Exaggerated attempts to project a command presence can make a would-be leader appear to be supercilious. Those who choose to project self-importance had better be exceptional performers. On the other hand, a manager who seems tentative and indecisive will not inspire confidence either. For example, a prior chapter lauded the value of possessing emotional intelligence. But not everyone is socially gracious. Different people possess differing levels of social empathy and have different thresholds of tolerance for errors committed by others. There is an apocryphal story that summarizes this point.

Olaf the Compassionate

It seems that a salty old supervisor by the name of Olaf had no patience for mistakes by his production crew. Especially unwelcome were errors that put stress on machine parts. Coming upon subordinates using equipment improperly, Olaf would turn red and begin to rant about "stupidity and people who didn't possess the brains that God gave geese." After witnessing one of Olaf's outbursts, his manager decided that Olaf needed human relations training and so he was dispatched for a two-week human relations training session in the Rocky Mountains.

Upon his first day back, Olaf was walking through the plant, going over his training in his head by repeating to himself, "nice and soft, warm and fuzzy, nice and soft, warm and fuzzy." Then Olaf came upon a piece of equipment belching smoke from its screeching bearings. Olaf quickly hit the emergency cut-off switch. Turning to the operator, Olaf shouted "Damn it Joe! When are you going to learn to lubricate the bearings? I swear you ain't got the brains God gave a goose." With that, Olaf stormed off to find his clipboard so he could document the incident. After two or three steps, Olaf remembered his training. Turning back to Joe he forced a smile and said, "By the way Joe, how are the wife and kids?"

Clearly, Olaf's human relations aspirations exceeded his grasp. Human relations theorists, moreover, are unrealistic to expect personality transformations, especially overnight. Most of us, of course, are milder than Olaf. Far greater percentages among us are in sync with Mary's desire that James would perform his job well without her having to engage in uncomfortable confrontation. Neither Olaf nor Mary can fundamentally change who they are. Nevertheless, a change in one's own behavior is a prerequisite to obtaining friction-free change in the behavior of subordinates. While Olaf's tirade might improve the employee's attention to machine maintenance, it might just as readily net him a punch in the nose from a subordinate who is more concerned about his personal dignity than keeping his job. Even if the employee is only chastened by the criticism and swallows his resentment, the damage can prove costly. Over time, the resentment produced by ill-treatment will long outlast the memory of the actual details of the encounter.

In the final analysis, a prerequisite to effective leadership is an understanding of power, both its acquisition and application. The power enjoyed by the leader stems from the authority that the organization assigns to the leader's position. Subordinates may quietly comply with one's wishes or challenge them due to fear of change or because they question the wisdom of the instruction or the leader's authority to issue it. When any of these occurs, managers who wish to be leaders should review the circumstances to formulate an appropriate response. Some prefer to compel compliance while others are more comfortable with persuasion or inspiration. An indispensable component, however, is the force of personality that underlies one's actions. Part of the reason why *they* comply is due to *who* is giving the order. Managers who know who they are and are willing to put their personal credibility and prestige behind a decision will come to find themselves looked upon as leaders.

Leaders and managers also benefit from applying the tools of effective communication. Clarity is the first responsibility of the leader. Clear, concise expectations that are stated sooner rather than later often make confrontation unnecessary because subordinates generally are no more comfortable with conflict than are supervisors. Some subordinates will respond with anger when they feel they are under attack, which is to be expected. Leaders who desire change rather than confrontation would do well to add the tools of effective communication to their skills repertoire.

Notes

[1] It is said that President Kennedy was so impressed with the book that he brought a first edition copy of *Presidential Power* (1960) to the White House.

[2] Truman, therefore, consulted members of his cabinet before making his decision. Included in the discussion was Secretary of State George Marshall, who had been the commander of both MacArthur and Eisenhower in World War II. Marshall strongly supported Truman's decision.

6

Ethics
The Dilemma of the Is and the Ought

> *" What is really good for me must turn out good for all, or else there is no good in the world at all. (John Dewey, 1891, p. 63)*
>
> *I would rather go to any extreme than suffer anything that is unworthy of my reputation, or that of my crown. (Queen Elizabeth I, quoted in Chamberlin, 1923, p. 161) "*

This chapter deals with questions of personal and organizational ethics, without which other leadership skills can lead to much evil in the world. In the final analysis, how one leads is as critical as where one leads.

The Bottom-Line Perspective

On the one hand, we have the modern management world with its principles of management, operations research, and managing to the bottom line. On the other hand, we have a body of literature that suggests that we create values-driven organizations. That is, organizations should define for themselves a core set of values that guide and inform their every action. Beginning with the techniques of management, there exists a set of universal principles that are applicable to all organizations and which are largely value-neutral. The second characteristic of modern management, operations research, encompasses the application of sophisticated computer models to control inventories, schedule shipments, and track work product. The third characteristic, managing to the bottom line, means decisions are based solely on their financial impacts. What is financially advantageous is what is right.

The more we have come to rely upon technology and formulas to assist decision making, the more we have moved away from the values component of decision making.

> ❝ *No amount of knowledge of the way the world is tells us how it ought to be, or what we ought to do . . . . The power or capacity to acquire knowledge is independent of moral character. There is nothing a good person can come to know, that a bad person cannot know, or come to know . . . . No fact is a value, no factual proposition entails an evaluative one. (The fact is that our society tends to dismiss values questions.) To call something a value judgment is tantamount to dismissing it as subjective. (Reeves, 1988, p. 115; emphasis added)* ❞

For example, in the last decade, financial managers came to rely on sophisticated mathematical models to determine appropriate financial risks in various investment strategies and in packaging classes of real estate assets to offer as collateral to leverage their credit worthiness in financial markets. The question in these deliberations was: Can we formulate these in such a way that they can withstand loan parameters used by lenders or those who manage the investment portfolios of others? The evidence suggests that decisions were frequently guided by profit projections and the potential impact of negative news on decision makers' bonus projections. The prudence of the strategies in terms of investor equity and long-term organizational health were lesser considerations.

In such a worldview, if something is not illegal per se, it is ok. Savvy managers who do not take advantage of the system by pressing the limits of what is legal are regarded by some as weak. Prudent decisions by managers are assumed to be somehow guaranteed by the realities of the market. Simply stated, the self-regulating market theory suggests that managers will not undertake unwarranted risks because to do so will jeopardize their place in the market should their exuberant risk taking not pan out. Unfortunately, such faith in the market's capacity for self-correction has been seriously undermined by events in 2008 (Greenspan, 2008).

By embracing the values approach, we are returning to the more traditional viewpoint in which it is just and proper to ask what is right as well as what is legal (Barrett, 2006). This is a departure from recent interpretations that view questions of right and wrong as mere value judgments that have no place in rational decision making. After thirty-plus years of studying and working in public organizations, this author applauds the return to values-based leadership and management because it is the best way of making the system work for the most people.

The Ethics Perspective

Since ancient times, the question of what is right has guided discussions of the behavior of individuals and organizations, whether public or private. Plato idealistically posited a state that would be run by the wisest and truest. Plato imagined that for the good of the state, the personal interests of these "philosopher kings" would never be put ahead of the good of the whole.

> 66 *Nor yet . . . does any other in any government whatever, so far as he is a governor, consider or dictate what is expedient for himself, but only for the governed and those to whom he acts as steward; and with an eye to this, and to what is expedient and suitable for this, he both says what he says, and does what he does. (Plato, 1901, p. 47)* 99

Of course, Plato hypothesized his perfect state such that it could be contrasted with the imperfection of the governing systems of Greece and the Mediterranean world at that time. He was not so naïve as to believe that such a state was practicable. As others note, the trouble with philosopher kings is their repeated inability to set aside their personal interests.

> 66 *The parochial consequence of giving the few wise and good power, is that they cease to remain wise and good. (John Dewey, quoted in Westbrook, 1991, p. 12)* 99

The problem is compounded by the fact that wise and good does not mean infallible. We therefore must not automatically assume that when they choose poorly that the choice is based on nefarious motives of personal gain. The American philosopher John Dewey (1891) posed a two-category framework of philosophy for judging actions. In one camp is the Kantian notion that people should be judged by the purity of their intentions rather than the outcome of their decisions. The other is the utilitarian framework of John Stuart Mill, who averred that the test of an act is its impact, especially on the many. As revealed in the chapter-opening quote, Dewey combines the two by suggesting that, in the final analysis, the good of the self depends on the impacts of one's actions on others.

Thus, for Dewey, the criterion for judging the motives underlying individual decision making should, in fact, be the impact on others. This truly profound statement is at the core of Dewey's worldview. If as humans we are merely engaged in a free-for-all struggle in which the winners write the history books and spin their motives however they choose, then human society is doomed. Western democracies have rejected the free-for-all option by embracing the rule of law precisely to create communities with standards of conduct by which all, the government as well as the governed, must abide. The mutuality of the self and the other is intensified because the actions of the many are limited relative to how they impact individuals. Thus, social covenants such as the U.S. Constitution are entered into as the guiding principles of the social order; they enable the collective while protecting the individual. The actual "rules of the game" are set out in legislative prescriptions. When cracks in the system allow the exclusively self-directed to manipulate the system to the detriment of the whole, the rules must be adapted to fit the current circumstance.

> 66 . . . government does now whatever experience permits or the times demand; though it does not do exactly the same thing as the ancient state. (Woodrow Wilson, 1898, p. 625) 99

Wilson succinctly describes American pragmatism, which calls for adaptation of the rules to the current circumstance—without departing from underlying values. But, it is a pragmatism guided by sustaining the greater good. The principle of constraint on individuals and groups is not limited to those who govern.

The conduct of private affairs, especially in American commerce, substantially rests on the premise of honesty and fair play. It is an underlying principle of American common law that when contracts are entered into, the parties are bound by *the covenant of good faith and fair dealing*. How binding this principle is has been interpreted differently by various courts. Nevertheless, that both parties will act openly and honestly and neither will seek advantage over the other through subterfuge or manipulation is a generally accepted principle (Burton, 1980). When one or both parties believe themselves to be wronged by the other, they have recourse to the court system.

The government cannot anticipate every ethical contingency nor can it formulate useful rules in which one size fits all. Attempting to do so has the potential for straitjacketing the freedom and innovation that makes the system work. In response to the Enron collapse that robbed investors and destroyed lives and careers, Congress passed the Sarbanes-Oxley Act (2002). Named for its authors, the act prescribes a regimen of openness and transparency that controls corporate mergers, new public offering of stock, or sales of publicly traded companies.

Each party to the transaction must demonstrate that it has acted with *due diligence* to disclose all relevant facts, such as pending lawsuits, location and value of assets, and any other contracts or indebtedness held by the company. The act was ad hoc in nature and designed to deal with a specific category of business transactions.

Thus, parties must not only act honestly, but demonstrate that they have taken every reasonable step to assure and document for others that they are doing so. Many a business leader has pointed to the cost of these labor-intensive regulations and lamented the fact that ethical businesses are saddled with the same expensive constraints as the unethical. And, at the end of the day, ethical organizations are not made more so by the process. Nevertheless, the manipulations of the unscrupulous have resulted in the regulation of all.

The development of ad hoc solutions to problems is quintessential American pragmatism. It reflects a conscious choice for situational rather than universal prescriptions. Furthermore, puritanical moral codes that cover every contingency and which societal members violate at their peril are impracticable. To the contrary, what is needed to maintain a well-functioning social order is an agreed-upon set of operating norms that are sufficiently rigorous to give us confidence that the actions of others are well intended, but that are sufficiently flexible to accommodate the variety of organizations that make up the current system.

Many public and private organizations have declined to wait for a universal code. Instead they have opted to devise their own ethical standards. They do so as a simple matter of business necessity. Here is an excerpt from a corporate ethics code grounded in pragmatism.

> A. For Cummins, ethics rests on a fundamental belief in people's dignity and decency. Our most basic ethical standard is to show respect for those whose lives we affect and to treat them as we would expect them to treat us if our positions were reversed . . .
>
> B. The reason for such behavior is that, in the long run, nothing else works. If economies and societies do not operate in this way, the whole machinery begins to collapse. No Corporation can long survive in situations where employees, creditors, and communities don't trust each other. (Cummins Engine Company, n.d.)

The Cummins example is representative of codes of ethics prescribed by individual corporations. Professions too are concerned with the personal conduct of their members. What follows are two excerpts taken from professional associations dedicated to serving the public interest.

> *These Principles . . . express the profession's recognition of its responsibilities to the public, to clients, and to colleagues. . . . The Principles call for an unswerving commitment to honorable behavior, even at the sacrifice of personal advantage. (American Institute of Certified Public Accountants, 2008/2009)*
>
> *. . . we, the members of the Society, commit ourselves to the following principles: . . . to serve the public interest; . . . respect the Constitution and the law; . . . demonstrate personal integrity; . . . promote ethical organizations; . . . strive for professional excellence. (American Society for Public Administration, 2006)*

The first is an association of professional specialists for whom integrity is the cornerstone of their business. The second is excerpted from the professional association dedicated to serving ethically in government.

American codes of ethics, whether generated as part of an organizational credo or that of a professional association, share the common theme of personal integrity. They correctly recognize that the support beam of an ethical organizational structure is the personal integrity of each of its members.

The mandate of ethical behavior falls first and heaviest on the shoulders of the leader. It is not enough to publicly embrace ethical conduct as an organizational credo. As noted elsewhere in this book, anybody can memorize and spout moral principles. Leaders who do not practice as well as preach ethics will soon learn that persons of integrity will not follow.

Returning to where we began, the issue of personal integrity is as timeless as organized society.

> *The consummate leader cultivates the Moral Law and strictly adheres to method and discipline, thus it is in his power to control success. (Sun Tzu, 1988, p. 20)*
>
> *Faced with what is right, to leave it undone shows a lack of courage. (Confucius, 1979, p. 66)*
>
> *A great prince should sooner put in jeopardy both his own interest and even those of the state than break his*

word, which he can never violate without losing his reputation and by consequence the greatest instrument of sovereigns. (Cardinal Richelieu, 1961, p. 102)

Particular justice is one part of general justice: it is the part which is concerned with the specific form of goodness which consists in behaving fairly or, as Aristotle called it, equally to other men. (Ross, 1998, p. 362)

Nor should integrity be confined to big public interactions that are watched by all. To cultivate ethics, the leader must manifest integrity in all manner of things, small as well as large. A Zen master once sent an acolyte to the market to purchase rice for the evening meal. Times were hard and funds were short, so the master admonished the novice to check with several dealers and bargain for the best possible price. Every dealer, however, quoted the young monk the same price. Finally the young man found one merchant who was very old and frail and who suffered from poor eyesight. Wanting to get home to his family, the old man quoted a price slightly lower than the others and the deal was struck. As the old man counted out the change, he mistakenly gave the young man five percent more change than necessary; thus a 5 percent discount became 10 percent. The young monk said nothing and returned to the monastery well pleased with his accomplishments. Proudly he proclaimed how the old man had erred as he handed over the change, which amounted to only a few cents. "Are you pleased with my service?" he asked. The master replied, "No I am not. You not only cheated an old man of his due but you sold your personal honor for a few cents. Well, I guess you know how much your honor is worth." With that, the young monk was dismissed from the monastery.

Leadership Development

> *The greatest commander of men was he whose intuitions most nearly happened. Nine-tenths of tactics were certain enough to be teachable in schools; but the irrational tenth was like the kingfisher flashing across the pool, and in it lay the tests of generals. (T. E. Lawrence, 1991/1926, p. 193)*
>
> *Trust yourself. Create the kind of self that you will be happy to live with all your life. Make the most of yourself by fanning the tiny, inner sparks of possibility into flames of achievement. (Golda Meir)*

Here we examine the challenge of leadership development from the perspective of organizations set on developing future leaders as well as from the point of view of those who aspire to lead. The discussion begins with the limits to leadership development in small organizations, then progresses to the challenges of leadership development in large organizations, using military and civilian examples. This is followed by a discussion of succession planning. The topic of selection for advancement is presented with an emphasis on the traits and competencies that organizations value. With the exception of organization founders and executives of proven ability recruited from the outside, rising to the rank of leader requires developing a support network, especially among one's superiors. The chapter closes with some suggestions for thinking and acting like a leader.

Leadership Development in Small Organizations

Small organizations (less than 25 members) are usually led by a single person. And while decision making may be delegated to facilitate operations, the authority to make fundamental change usually is not. Subordinates who make prudent decisions are promoted and their duties expanded as the organization grows and as individuals demonstrate a capacity for increased responsibility. Training is on the job and ad hoc; frequently the subordinate learns operating procedures and priorities within the organization on a need-to-know basis. These might include such responsibilities as how to make a bank deposit, what the owner considers appropriate sales call comportment, and the proper way to correct the behavior of subordinates. Leadership development and succession planning are rare, with the possible exception of family-run enterprises whose founder is nearing retirement. These decisions are very likely to be made on the basis of kinship rather than merit. Salesperson A may demonstrate much more potential than the owner's son, salesperson B. But the smart money would bet on B as the most likely successor. Whoever is tapped will be required to learn the ins and outs of operational financing and balancing inventories, how to be an effective liaison with external actors such as customers and suppliers, and the critical function of monitoring competitors for price competitiveness and product innovation. The foregoing say nothing of the vision, leadership, and organizational skills necessary for success of enterprises large and small.

Leadership Development in Large Organizations

Very large organizations that number in the hundreds and thousands may or may not maintain comprehensive development programs. The various branches of the United States military provide excellent examples of detailed infrastructures that are in place to ensure a comprehensive approach to leadership selection and development.

The U.S. Military

The foundation of officer corps development is four years of academic training combined with socialization into the rituals, language, and customs of military life at the United States military academies. The academies offer rigorous academic curricula taught by both military and civilian faculty. Discipline and socialization of cadets and midshipmen are done by upperclassmen. The values of duty, honor, and loyalty are reinforced on a daily basis along with the necessity of obedience to orders and responsibility for the performance and well-being of others.

Officer corps development at the academies is supplemented by the ROTC (Reserve Officer Training Corps) on college campuses. ROTC students pursue a variety of academic disciplines and also develop military skills through didactic classroom study, rigorous physical training, and summer sessions of formal military training.

Finally, promising enlisted personnel are offered the opportunity to move up from the ranks of noncommissioned officers through officer candidate school. The military systematically tests new recruits for academic achievement in math and science, general intelligence, and special gifts such as mechanical aptitude and the potential for learning foreign languages. Intellectually gifted, low-ranking enlisted personnel are sometimes invited to leave the ranks and attend the academies.

Newly minted officers other than pilots and other technically skilled specialties are normally assigned as supervisors over operational units as small as 15 to 25 troops. Their leadership and decision making are watched closely by more senior officers, much like at the academies. Brand-new second lieutenants supervise troops not much younger than themselves. Thus, inspiring confidence in their leadership and decision making on the part of subordinates must be accomplished without the natural deference that age sometimes provides. The performance of these young officers is critically important to mission success and they are held directly responsible for the conduct and often the lives of others.

To assist in these challenging endeavors, each lieutenant is assigned a group of noncommissioned officers (NCOs). The most senior of these can play a critical role in helping the supervisor succeed or at the very least prevent critical errors. "Listen to your gunny," (gunnery sergeant) is the best advice that a marine corps captain can give a new lieutenant. The "gunny" or army/air force "top" sergeant or navy "chief" petty officer see to operational details and enforce discipline.

> " *Everything I know about leadership, I learned from a chief petty officer. (Senator John McCain, second televised presidential debate with Senator Barack Obama, October 7, 2008)* "

When fully utilized, NCOs can make an officer look good—even a reluctant officer such as Tobias Wolff during his tour of duty as a Green Beret captain in support of Vietnamese troops during the 1968 Tet Offensive:

> " *For eleven months we had lived together. Each morning Sergeant Benet had appeared in fresh fatigues, with our day already mapped out. He called me sir. He found work for us to do when there didn't seem to be any and somehow let me know what orders I should give him to preserve the fiction of my authority. I knew that he was*

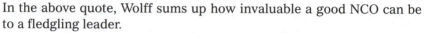

my superior in every way that mattered, but he didn't allow me to acknowledge this and gave no sign of suspecting it himself. (Wolff, 1994, p. 196)

In the above quote, Wolff sums up how invaluable a good NCO can be to a fledgling leader.

From an organization perspective, NCOs are the backbone of the organization. Their attention to detail facilitates an officer's attempts to lead and succeed. What should never be overlooked is the reality that, in times of uncertainty, particularly when there is a potential for physical danger or repercussions from above, young soldiers will look to their senior peers (the NCOs) for leadership on whether or not, or how fast, to obey the orders of commissioned officers.

In terms of leadership development, lower-level success can engender an eagerness for more responsibility. Those who show promise are singled out for advanced training in military tactical skills, doctrine, and history. Ultimately, their responsibilities are extended over larger numbers of troops. And, because the peer group narrows as they ascend the ranks, those of lesser promise, by necessity, are encouraged to leave the service.

Civilian Organizations

Civilian organizations also seek to recruit, train, and promote people with leadership potential and problem-solving skills. Most organizations, however, lack the formal infrastructure found in the military. Some organizations set expectations, then leave first-line managers to sink or swim on their own merits. Few organizations, moreover, have the good sense or resources to assign potential leaders to supervise the civilian version of top quality noncommissioned officers. Ironically, a unit supervisor in a civilian organization may find that his or her first decision is to select a successor for a retiring NCO.

The civilian equivalents of NCOs include the echelon just below management, comprised of working supervisors. Elsewhere we distinguished between those responsible for work production and those tasked with organizational planning who also exercise financial responsibility. Other civilian equivalents of the NCO include lead persons in factories, office managers, senior clerical personnel, and so forth. The author's own task as a manager was greatly assisted by a senior secretary who reminded him of deadlines from above and identified developing problems among professional staff. Further, her institutional memory of organization policies, procedures, and interpersonal dynamics proved invaluable.

Highly technical organizations find it doubly important to train supervisors and managers because they are prone to overemphasize technical competencies rather than leadership potential when recruiting and promoting. Recognizing this failing, some forward thinking technical organizations engage in training partnerships with nearby universities to provide advanced managerial training on-site at company facilities. Trainees are sometimes allowed to take classes during working hours, but a more common model involves evening and weekend study. Whether classes are taught during or outside working hours, the employers generally pay the cost of training. Similar initiatives have been undertaken by public organizations through tuition reimbursement programs. It is a rare government organization, however, that possesses the resources to pay 100 percent of the education costs for developing its managers.

The U.S. Office of Personnel Management (OPM) operates the Federal Executive Institute through which federal executives at the upper ranks of management (GS 15 and above)[1] may take seminars and workshops. These classes are designed to enhance their leadership competence in anticipation of promotion into the upper ranks of the Federal Executive Service. Individuals nominate themselves for this training. Selection, however, can be highly competitive. And since the required rank for consideration is that of GS 15, one must have already demonstrated considerable managerial and leadership potential to have risen that far from the normal entry level for professional grades (GS 7 to 9). OPM also offers a variety of training and developmental seminars for managers of lower ranks who wish to improve their skills. Unfortunately, such elaborate systems as those available to U.S. military and civilian agencies are quite beyond the reach of most corporations as well as most states and virtually all county and municipal government employers.

Succession Planning

Executive development has moved to the forefront of the public management literature as agencies struggle to find ways to cope with the upcoming retirement of a generation of senior executives. The federal government estimates that 70 percent of its senior executives are eligible for retirement. This all too familiar challenge is identified as succession planning, which is an artifact of government traditions of long-term, stable employment. Many public managers spend their entire career in a single agency, so organizations can go years without thinking about who should be next in line for executive positions. Recent studies suggest that an alarming number of senior level public-sector executives who began their careers in the 1970s or 1980s have reached the age of retirement. These agencies find themselves scrambling to identify and advance promising mid-level managers into the ranks of the executives (PricewaterhouseCoopers, 2006).

Systematic Training

The challenge to such agencies is how to develop an executive perspective among their most promising mid-level managers. Unfortunately, promise is just that—promise. Intelligence and eagerness must be leavened with experience. One approach is to enhance the job responsibilities of trainees by adding tasks that normally are assigned to higher grades. The goal is to bridge their current responsibilities and those of the position for which they are being targeted.

Executive development can involve advanced academic training. Entry into the professional ranks of the public service requires a bachelor's degree. Before advancing very far, however, the preferred credential is a master's degree, preferably but not exclusively in public administration. Many government agencies provide tuition-assistance programs, but these rarely have kept pace with the increasing costs of tuition. Organizations with a commitment to leadership development and the resources to appropriately fund it should allocate resources for training and development that specifically target the organization's needs. Simple tuition reimbursement programs, for example, may enhance the intellectual abilities of the participant and prepare them for alternative career choices, but provide little benefit to the organization. For example, sending police officers to graduate school to major in creative writing so they can become crime writers does little to meet the command needs of the police department. On the other hand, a mixture of leadership training seminars, job-relevant academic training, and bridging jobs can maximize the benefits from their developmental dollar.

Another developmental device is the technique known as "shadowing," wherein the trainee spends a period of time with a qualified executive observing and listening to the decision-making process. If he or she is lucky, the executive being shadowed will challenge the trainee to provide solutions to the various problems that arise, discuss the various options and their ramifications, and also explain the rationale upon which the actual decision is based. Furthermore, the trainee can gather valuable insights by observing how the executive presents the decision to subordinates and how he or she deals with subordinate reactions.

Smaller governmental agencies do not have broad enough hierarchies to facilitate the shadowing process. These smaller units of government can enter into cooperative arrangements with adjacent jurisdictions whereby agencies deploy their mid-level managers to work in the other agency for on-the-job training. This sharing of resources has the added advantage of expanding the worldview of the parent organization because the trainees gain insights and perspectives and are able to observe systems not in use in their parent organization. It is often the case that the cooperating organization has innovative approaches that are highly transferable to the parent organization.

Mentoring

The most ancient and time-honored method of leadership development is the use of a mentor. These programs take the name from the original "Mentor" of Greek mythology who, as the loyal servant of Odysseus, saw to the development of the latter's son Talemacus (Homer, 1906). Before the advent of the vaunted English public schools (which are in reality exclusive private academies), members of the gentry would send their children to be trained as knights and potential rulers by a trusted vassal. The presumed advantage to vassal-training was that it ensured that the young charge would be subjected to the hard work and discipline necessary to becoming a powerful and wise ruler. The sage Confucius is quoted as having said, "How can you say you love someone and not teach them to work hard?" The vassal system ensured that the training discipline would not be undermined by parental indulgence. Subsequent generations of the nobility sent their children off to the so-called public schools. There the children learned academic skills, required behavior, and so forth far from parental supervision. Lord Wellington is alleged to have said in the aftermath of his historic victory over Napoléon, "the Battle of Waterloo was won on the playing fields of Eton." At their public schools, the English gentry learned to play hard, persevere under stress, and to cooperate in the face of adversity (see Holmes, 2003).

Much has been written about the benefits of mentor programs in modern organizations (see Douglas, 1997). The idea is that an up-and-coming leader benefits from the advice and counsel of a more seasoned manager. The problem is that many organizations do not have enough senior mentors for everybody who needs training. Mentorship, moreover, requires interpersonal bonding, which is as much a matter of personality as it is good advice and counsel. When bonding does not occur, the mentor relationship can become pro forma and a mere drain on the time of both individuals.

Some of the best mentor-mentee relationships grow spontaneously out of a mutual liking on the part of individuals. These natural mentorships can involve persons of varying ranks who provide guidance and assistance that is balanced against necessary protocol and rank deference. Formal mentor programs can have difficulty making optimal matches. Young female managers, for example, may find themselves in an organizational culture of male dominance where few senior females are available with whom to bond. This is not to suggest that male executives cannot mentor female managers; however, they are more likely to form social relationships with male subordinates outside of work merely due to mutual interests in such things as sports competitions and hobbies such as golf. Of course, many executives make the training of subordinates an integral part of their duties and responsibilities. But this is more aptly called training rather than mentoring.

A much more frequent circumstance in organizations without formal mentor programs is for fledgling leaders to consult older family members and friends. These mentorships have the added advantage of being completely outside the chain of command and therefore immune from organizational politics. The mentee can also be assured that the act of seeking help will not reflect badly upon his or her judgment or decisiveness. That said, mentors within the hierarchy have an additional value.

> But on this business of who you know, a one-minute lecture to any young person who may read these words:
>
> Always try to associate yourself closely with and learn as much as you can from those who know more than you, who do better than you, who see more clearly than you. Don't be afraid to reach upward. Apart from the rewards of friendship, the association might pay off at some unforeseen time—that is only an accidental by-product. The important thing is that the learning will make you a better person. (Former President and Five Star General Dwight Eisenhower, 1967, pp. 200–201)

Selection for Advancement

Very large organizations often set up elaborate processes for reviewing and documenting performance that contain an explicit assessment of promotion potential. Promotion per se may be handled by panels of senior officials (such as in the military) that regularly meet to advance entire cohorts of the worthy. More common in the civilian sector is ad hoc advancement as needs arise. In either case, the goal is to identify and advance the most meritorious. In reality, however, pure merit is often compromised by institutional values and personal relationships. In the military, for example, a predisposition exists to advance academy graduates over reserve officers. In addition, in both civilian and military organizations, advantage is often gained through the sponsorship of more senior officials with social ties to one of the candidates. Unfair as this may seem, it is a truth with roots in ancient traditions that merit advocates must fight to overcome:

> *Promote those you do recognize. Do you suppose others will allow those you fail to recognize to be passed over? (Confucius, 1979, p. 118)*

What the sage is warning against here is vacillation over whom to select. He was in fact one of the world's earliest advocates of merit systems, having himself risen from relative poverty and without social network sponsorship. What Confucius is urging is to promote those whose merits you readily see. Others will recognize those you may have missed. Taking our cue from the sage, when we are called upon to participate in a selection or promotion process where a particular candidate in our view is superior, we have an obligation to become that person's advocate against those who prefer another candidate for not so meritorious reasons.

Who Are the Potential Leaders? How to Get Chosen?

The identification/selection question is as relevant for those who wish to become leaders as it is for organizations seeking to identify them. In today's job market, education credentials are necessary as thresholds that normally must be cleared. One need only look at professional-level job announcements that specify a minimum of a bachelor's degree. In many cases, post-employment advancement requires the obtainment of a master's degree as a prerequisite for consideration. There are, of course, glaring exceptions of individuals of enormous talent who succeeded without the normal credentials. An example is Bill Gates, who dropped out of college to start Microsoft. But a job search visit to that company's Web site will reveal that it, too, has a bias toward education credentials.

Credentials, however, are a threshold (a minimum qualification) that in and of themselves will not guarantee advancement. Nevertheless, they do indicate a certain level of organization and attention to self-development. What follows are suggestions that would-be leaders may wish to follow to enhance their potential for getting noticed beyond their basic education credentials.

> *My grandfather once told me that there are two kinds of people: those who work and those who take the credit. He told me to try to be in the first group; there was less competition there. (Indira Gandhi)*

Task competence. First and foremost, organizations are most likely to promote people who are good at their current jobs. The duties and responsibilities that an employee currently performs can demonstrate initiative, innovation, work planning, and attention to detail. If you are good they will notice. Historians tell us that Alexander Hamilton, who as George Washington's secretary of the treasury was the architect of the nation's banking and financial system, began his rise to prominence by distinguishing himself as an officer in the Continental Army. The performance of his artillery batteries was well-ordered and disciplined during the Continental Army's rout at the hands of British troops during the fall of New York. Very soon, the plucky commander found himself on Washington's staff, where Hamilton's energy and genius for the written word soon led to his taking principal responsibility for all of Washington's communications with the Congress and other field commanders (Chernow, 2004).

Hamilton's natural gifts and stupendous intellect would doubtlessly have led to success even if there had been no Revolutionary War. Nevertheless, selection of officers in militias was by popular vote. Many officers cared more for status and maintaining popularity with the troops than they did for war preparation. Hamilton, by contrast, eschewed popularity for hard training and discipline. The primary dividend of this task competence was a combat-ready unit. The secondary benefit was the notice of his superiors.

One can, in fact, demonstrate task competence that leads to advancement even while working under a manager with a penchant for hogging all the credit. General and President Dwight Eisenhower was once asked if he was familiar with the flamboyant style of General Douglas MacArthur, his counterpart in the Pacific during World War II. He responded that he had indeed had the opportunity to study MacArthur close-up or as he put it "to understudy him" for eight years, first at the Pentagon and then in the Philippines. There, the two looked to the geographic and technical challenges that would be presented by an anticipated Japanese invasion. During these years, Lt. Col. Eisenhower demonstrated insight, initiative, and loyalty, the latter being the military virtue most dear to MacArthur (Manchester, 1978). At the same time MacArthur, already a four star general with a legendary ego and personal flamboyance, sucked all the air out of any room he entered—yet Eisenhower managed to get noticed. Whatever the organization, extreme competence is hard to overlook.

The virtues of volunteering. Those responsible for identifying new leaders will first look to those who have distinguished themselves in some meaningful way. But, this is easier said than done in large organizations engaged in routine tasks. In this regard the most untrue of all axioms is "never, ever volunteer." This saying no doubt stems from one of Murphy's laws. According to Murphy, "The frequency with which one will be asked to engage in highly dangerous activities will be proportional to the success that one demonstrates in performing them."[2] So, for example, low-level soldiers who demonstrate great skill in charging enemy machine-gun nests will find themselves asked to perform the task over and over.

In stark contrast to proponents of the never-volunteer thesis are those who step up to volunteer for tasks that others may not even recognize as critical. Returning to the example of Eisenhower's advancement, his position as principal assistant to MacArthur would have guaranteed him a role of substance in the Pacific theater of the war he and MacArthur saw coming. Instead, Ike sought and received permission to return to the United States from the Philippines to help rebuild American forces (Eisenhower, 1967, p. 231). By volunteering, he moved out from under MacArthur's shadow and patronage into the view of War Department officials scrambling to prepare for war. When the time came to select a commander for American troops in the European theater, Eisenhower was selected over many senior officers (Manchester, 1978).

Civilian organizations both public and private also welcome volunteers. When special work groups or task forces are formed to address specific problems outside of routine operations, those who step up and volunteer are very likely to be selected. It should hardly be necessary to point out that task forces are formed to carry out the priorities of top management. Success in these venues, then, is success in achieving the priority goals of top management. In terms of getting noticed, high-level executives are much more likely to attend task force meetings that address their priorities than they are to attend routine staff sessions where ordinary work performance is assessed. But, it should be borne in mind that selection for special projects is generally reserved for those who have demonstrated task competence. Thus, task competence can lead to selection for special duties that in turn will lead to notice by superiors.

Energy and enthusiasm. Volunteering for special operations allows one to demonstrate high energy. The reasoning goes that the volunteer performs his or her routine tasks with little fuss and high efficiency, with time left over to do the extras. Obviously, volunteering is not attractive to those who are overwhelmed by their current duties and responsibilities; nor should one volunteer if one has a myriad of life commitments outside the work organization. Finding a balance between work and life is a difficulty shared by everyone. The simple reality is that people who wish to rise to the top must make a commitment to do more within the organization and to do it without complaint.

Probity. When superiors ask subordinates for their views regarding how to proceed with a particular problem or project, the query should be taken as an initial vote of confidence in the subordinates' judgment, or at the very least a test thereof. Such requests are an opportunity to demonstrate probity. Recalling chapter 4, one should bear in mind the necessity for careful consideration of the options as well as the need to be decisive. For example, an elementary school principal might be asked to chair a task force on integrating computer learning into the district's curriculum. Before scheduling presentations by various sales representatives from computer hardware and software companies, probity would suggest the following. Part of the inquiry should be to study other schools that have adapted their curricula for best practices. It is almost never necessary to reinvent the wheel. Those in charge of maintaining computer learning facilities should be queried as to the level of utilization and current capacity. The working group should also consult with classroom teachers regarding their perceptions of how computers might be integrated into the curriculum, and teachers should be asked to assess themselves regarding their competence in utilizing the computer for teaching purposes.

Over the course of the group's consultations one should always come to meetings prepared to discuss the matter at hand. Regular task force members should not hesitate to express their views regarding the various options under consideration. All such views should, however, be expressed without rancor and in a manner that demonstrates age- and rank-appropriate respect for other members of the group. How the chairperson of the work group comports him or herself while expressing a personal viewpoint is vitally important. The chair sets the tone as well as the agenda. A chairperson who expresses his or her views too forcefully, especially early on in the discussion, risks stifling alternative points of view. Early and assertive articulations of the leader's view can rightly or wrongly give the impression that the leader is expressing organizational doctrine and that critical decisions have all been made. When this happens, enthusiasm in the task force will be quickly squashed.

A more prudent role for the leader is to act as a facilitator of the discussion. Individuals with good ideas but mild personalities can have their ideas overridden by lesser ideas stated in a firm manner. The chair should thus facilitate the discussion by attempting to draw out every member for views on the various topics. After everyone has been heard, the leader should facilitate a transition in the discussion from what *could* be done to what *should* be done. Normally, this entails a search for the middle ground between wish list and what can be carried forward to senior managers. What the group recommends is probably as much a function of funding availability as it is of the intrinsic value of the various options. The chair should keep this consideration front and center as a rubric for the discussion of recommendations.

Returning to our computer task force example, probity mandates taking the middle path. Absent a windfall of funding from a philanthropic organization or an unanticipated bout of generosity on the part of the legislature, the middle is what is possible. If a windfall were to occur, the district would benefit by bringing in some expensive consultants from the major hardware vendors who, no doubt, could also provide software training for staff. This might entail replacing all current computers with the new system and a comprehensive summer training program for teachers.

A far more likely scenario, however, is that the group will be asked to make recommendations on how to spend highly limited discretionary funds. It is entirely possible that the group would learn that many of the teachers lack training on the integration of computers into their teaching. If so, the current computer capacity may well be underutilized. Thus, recommendations that involved focusing on curriculum development and teacher competence would go a long way toward a least-cost solution to the district's problems. If these recommendations were combined with suggestions for replacing obsolete computers first, while upgrading the software of newer models, the task force recommendations would be much more likely to be accepted.

In a year of limited budgets and belt-tightening, if one pushed for radical alterations to the status quo, the ideas in all likelihood would fall against the barrier of practicality. From the standpoint of personal advancement, moreover, those pushing the extreme recommendations may be lauded for their energy and passion. They will not, however, be thought of as prudent or creative. Successful management, particularly in the public sector, is the art of achieving what is possible rather than imagining the ideal.

Building a Network

An earlier quote from Eisenhower articulated his view on the importance of building networks in order to learn and advance. Also worth repeating is the truism that small talk and affability do not come naturally to many people. Nevertheless, how one treats others will contribute greatly to one's future success. The day-to-day business of work can have as much impact on an individual's advancement as the results achieved.

> ❝ *At court, when speaking with Counselors of lower rank he was affable; when speaking with Counselors of upper rank, he was frank though respectful. In the presence of his lord, his bearing, though respectful, was composed. (Confucius, 1979, p. 101)* ❞

The foregoing prescription by the sage suggests a comportment that is a synthesis of emotional intelligence, probity, and command presence. In dealing with subordinates, one need not flaunt rank to inspire the respect and deference to authority that is intrinsic in most people. Affability, defined as a pleasant, approachable demeanor, will empower subordinates to report rather than hide problems and to be forthcoming with suggestions when needed.

In dealing with superiors, how frankly one expresses views should be calibrated to the affability of the superior and the working relationship that has been established—especially when one's opinion has not been sought. But as Confucius suggests, when asked, one should be frank yet respectful. A very wise bureaucrat once advised this author that when dealing with council members (read: superiors), "you never want to let them know that you think you are smarter than them—regardless of how self-evident the difference might be." Superiors who are treated with condescension are very likely to say no, at the very least. At worst, they have been known to retaliate when made to feel inferior. Arrogance and egotism are traits often associated with artistic genius, the product of which compensates for the artist's comportment. They are not attractive traits in ordinary mortals.

In the presence of those of the highest authority ("in the presence of his lord"; read: CEO/commanding officer), the capacity to simultaneously exude confidence and respectfulness is a skill that is not easily learned. One should resist the impulse to compensate for discomfort by making wisecracks, regardless of whether "the lord" seems amused. Moreover, stammering responses to direct queries do not inspire confidence. This pitfall can be avoided, for the most part, by carefully preparing for the meeting—anticipate what will be asked and pre-think the answers. Taking a moment to formulate one's response lends itself to succinctness of speech that both conveys composure and moves the discussion along. Bear in mind that your work product is rarely the only priority demanding the boss's attention.

Confucius does not cover lateral relationships in his comportment advice. Perhaps the sage presumed their inclusion in the rules of proper comportment, or he may have thought them to be a matter of ordinary civility. We simply cannot know his intent at this late date. Peer relations in the modern era, however, are as critical as appropriate behavior towards one's organizational superiors.

To begin with, it costs nothing to acknowledge good performance on the part of peers. Nor does it hurt to praise them when they have good ideas. Their performance does not diminish one's own achievements. A lack of hubris toward peers, moreover, is doubly noticeable when they do not reciprocate. Those who sneer and denigrate the thinking of others appear jealous and insecure—not superior.

More importantly, networks with peers can form the foundation for a future supportive constituency. More than a few politicians shook their heads in wonder at the rolodex of Bill Clinton, whose interpersonal skills and networking while governor of a small state eventually formed the foundation for his successful presidential bid.

Perhaps most important is the fact that friendly, cooperative relations with organization peers are essential to the performance of daily tasks; that is, task competence. Regardless of one's level of personal magnetism, personal intelligence, and so forth, high-level productivity flows from groups of individuals working together. This holds true no matter how good one's ideas are. Leadership is getting others to embrace and implement one's ideas. Ignoring this reality can sacrifice productivity and engender resentment.

Graciousness

One's peers may be the competition for organization advancement, but there is no need to be cutthroat about it. The operating mode of Japanese corporate culture is significant in this regard. When faced with a problem, Japanese managers set about defining it and searching for solutions. By contrast, in American corporate culture, personal insecurity over not wanting to look bad in front of the bosses often combines with individual competitiveness to produce intense sessions dedicated to fixing the blame rather than finding solutions. At a minimum, solutions are delayed. At worst, the enmity generated by these sessions can turn a well-organized work group into a dysfunctional family in which personal resentments, intense emotions, and the desire to "get even" can lead to willful neglect of duties and even sabotage by those who feel slighted. Like dysfunctional families whose members become estranged and/or divorced, bickering and backbiting between peers can lead to dissolution of the work group and involuntary separations from the organization.

The Japanese Way

The Japanese embrace the principle of group cooperation and achievement. And yet, the exceptional get noticed despite Japan's penchant for personal modesty; a preference carried to such extremes that individuals are embarrassed to the point of mortification when singled out for personal praise in front of their peers. Credit for quality performance is celebrated as a group achievement. The group is also responsible for achieving solutions. How, one might ask, are leaders selected for advancement in Japanese organizations if individual performances are not the standard? In fact they are the standard, but organization superiors are so involved with the performance of the group that they know who is and is not contributing, who has a good idea and who does not. Those who do are advanced ahead of their peers.

Japanese Modesty

In 1963 I had the honor of making the acquaintance of a 23-year-old Japanese college graduate who had come to the United States to teach judo and to practice his English. Being the same age, we made friends quickly, and while he was tossing me and my cohorts around, I learned a great deal about his background and aspirations. First, in college he was captain of his university judo team. In Japan, the captain is elected by the team members and takes responsibility for training, conditioning, and motivating the other athletes. This stands in contrast to the United States, where captains are often designated by coaches and perform the function of calling coin tosses and choosing end zones.

My cohorts and I were curious as to why this obviously talented man did not immediately go into business. He said he wanted to give back to judo, which had given him so much, and he wanted to become fluent in English to help his career. We had difficulty understanding this because none of us was interested in learning any foreign language. At that time, the great importation of Japanese cars, televisions, and other consumer products had not yet begun. At any rate, he remained in a small California town for two years where he learned how to socialize with Americans. He also learned how to drive a car, chase women, and to hunt small game. After he left, we continued to write back and forth over the years.

His first letter indicated that he had taken a job for a large import/export company and was living in a company dormitory for low-level managers. Two years later a letter came from the Philippines, where his job assignment was to purchase pigs from rural farmers in areas so remote and dangerous that he had to carry a sidearm. His work was made possible because of his English, and he was also grateful for our teaching him how to drive a car and shoot a gun.

Two years later, he was purchasing lumber in Southeast Asia that was shipped to Japan and the United States. In another two years, he wrote that he was moving to Los Angeles where he would be deputy manager for U.S. sales. He returned to Japan a couple of years later and we lost touch.

Twenty years later I sought to reconnect with him when my work took me to Japan on various teaching assignments. I called the San Francisco headquarters of his last known employer in a Hail Mary attempt to contact him. The operator asked me his name and immediately gave me his Tokyo contact information. When we met for lunch in Tokyo he was characteristically reluctant to list his achievements. He said he was nearing retirement and looking forward to more time with his family. His career had advanced with promotions every couple of years, much faster than is normally the case in Japanese companies whose hierarchies are flat and advancement slow. I still could not gauge from his reporting how far this modest man had advanced. That evening I asked a translator in my class to read me his business card. It read: Chief Executive Officer, International Lumber Division, of one of the world's biggest import/export companies.

The lesson to be learned is that this person's potential was recognized from an early age by his peers and superiors alike. His advance up the hierarchy was steady and well ahead of the norm. He achieved this apparently without engaging in self-aggrandizement or speaking ill of others who might have competed with him.

> ❝ *The race is not always to the swift nor the battle to the strong, but that's the way to bet it. (Damon Runyon, 1952)* ❞

Thinking and Acting like a Leader

There are two critical components to leadership preparation. Developing the mind-set of leadership is critical to achieving long-term success in organizations. Intelligence cannot be taught. It either exists or it does not, but intellect can be honed and focused. Second, one must equip oneself with the skill set of executives.

> ❝ *Nothing is more necessary in governing a state than foresight, since by its use one can easily prevent many evils which can be corrected only with great difficulty if allowed to transpire. (Cardinal Richelieu, 1961, p. 80)*
>
> *To fill our heads, like a scrapbook, with this and that item as a finished and done-for thing, is not to think. It is to turn ourselves into a piece of registering apparatus. To consider the bearing of the occurrence upon what may be, but is not yet, is to think. (John Dewey, 1949, p. 58)* ❞

The Habit of Thinking Strategically

An apt trait to develop is to routinely step back from day-to-day pressures and try to understand internal work flows and think about how systems can be improved. Second, review trends and movements in the environment of the organization. Remember, those at the top must balance their attention between operational and external factors. Problems must be anticipated and the groundwork laid in order to sustain and grow the organization. Thus, for example, an organization that is committed to employee development and is anticipating rapid growth through the establishment of new operational units, should anticipate the need for training and development of leaders from among the ranks of existing employees before recruiting from outside.

> ❝ *The artisan, in any of the hundred crafts, masters his trade by staying in his workshop; the gentleman perfects his way through learning. (Confucius, 1979, p. 154)* ❞

History has much to teach us about self-development. General Douglas MacArthur, for example, spent long hours every day studying the history of warfare strategies that worked and those that failed. To use a modern-day phrase, MacArthur was constantly in search of the "best practices" of warfare. He studied developments in weapons and tactics and was quick to adapt his own fighting strategies with the advent of airpower. MacArthur also worked very hard to understand the culture and motivation of nations that were potential enemies.

Much has been written about his brilliance as a tactician and the victories that he won while minimizing his own casualties. His leadership greatness, however, is perhaps best reflected in his governorship of a defeated Japan. His first strategic priority was to advance America's long-term interests in the Far East. MacArthur arrived at his post with a set of strategic objectives designed to supplant Japan's feudal/warrior culture with a modern democracy. Thus, one of his priorities in drafting the constitution of postwar Japan was to give women the vote. MacArthur was not moved by the spirit of feminism but by a personal recognition that women by and large are opposed to war and their empowerment would temper Japanese tendencies in that direction. MacArthur's governorship of occupied Japan was mild rather than punitive, and sought to repair that nation's infrastructure and develop its manufacturing industries while at the same time advancing democratic institutions. In MacArthur's view the goal was not so much the pacification of Japan as it was advancing America's interests in that region of the world, which he predicted would become critical in world affairs.

It is also worth noting that the general had thought through how he would govern occupied Japan well before final victory was achieved. With 20-20 hindsight we can now see that MacArthur was not only right about the future of the region but also highly successful in converting Japan to a democratic, industrialized nation strategically aligned with the United States.

Education

The first rule of education is that it is never complete. A Zen adage sums up this point nicely.

> ❝ *If you die tonight, learn something new today.* ❞

Humans are by nature adaptive creatures. Survival dictated that we learn from our mistakes. Those who did not perished or failed to thrive. Put another way, learning from one's experience and constantly remaining on the alert for new information are good predictors of success. Knowledge and adaptation have been the hallmarks of human survival through the millennia. Internalizing and interpreting new facts and situations and then integrating them into one's thinking patterns are the beginning of wisdom. Those who cannot learn cannot lead, at least not for very long.

The leadership of modern organizations requires the acquisition of very specific skill sets for processing information. Top leadership requires the ability to read and interpret financial data, period. Those who do not understand the basics of finance and its language will generally fall prey to those who do. This is not to suggest that one must be an exceptional bean counter to become an executive. But schooling in the basics of accounting and financial reporting is essential. One cannot expect to become a division chief if one cannot do the numbers. Normally, reading and interpreting a spreadsheet and being able to critically analyze and discuss financial planning models are gateway skills to the executive floor. They are not in and of themselves sufficient to secure advancement.

Decisiveness

Chapter 4 treated decision making in depth. Here the intent is to connect the dots with the other skills noted above. Effective decision making is one part reasoning, one part knowledge, and one part decisive action. Those seasoned by experience may recognize a particular organizational challenge as a recurring theme in organizations.

 Plus ça change plus sont le même chose.

The phrase "the more things change the more they stay the same," is often delivered with a knowing nod of the head by cynical economics professors or with a sigh by disappointed consumers faced with price increases despite government promises to the contrary. Treating a recurring problem in an organization as something in need of a thoughtful remedy is a trait of leadership.

Faced with what is right, to leave it undone shows a lack of courage. (Confucius, 1979, p. 66)

Begin by assessing the problem to the best of your abilities, bringing to bear your intellect, experience, and knowledge of organizational history. State your position clearly and specify the actions you want taken. Approach the task with enthusiasm and energy and hold others responsible for completing projects as ordered.

Lessons to Be Taken

Let us conclude where we started. Leaders are not born knowing instinctively what needs to be done. Nor do they have an innate sense of how to treat others. Factual knowledge can be learned, while experience can be the best teacher if we choose to learn from it. Poor life choices can be altered. Inappropriate reactions to others can be reviewed and integrated into one's experiential frame of reference to forestall a recurrence of the poor choice. Skill in balancing between short- and long-term priorities can be honed. So too can one learn to examine issues in terms of their primary and secondary outcomes. Decide promptly and move forward with resolve.

Learning to calculate and avoid unnecessary risks also is a skill well worth cultivating by would-be leaders. Unfortunately, the anxiety that risk and uncertainty provoke in individuals varies greatly—based, in no small part, on the individual's neurological makeup. Fighter pilots, motocross racers, quarterbacks, and skydivers may be blessed with an abundance of serotonin such that they do not physically experience fear like the rest of us. This can be a significant advantage for those providing leadership in dangerous situations where decisions must be made quickly and the consequences of inaction are grave. Of course, there can be devastating effects when prudence is overridden by aggressiveness—bear in mind General Custer.

Regardless, one must calculate his or her own comfort level with risk and factor it into decision making. One's personal anxieties cannot be allowed to immobilize the many who are dependent on one's leadership. General Douglas MacArthur consistently took calculated risks that saved lives and brought victory. But that does not mean he was immune to anxiety, despite his two Congressional Medals of Honor. At the outset of the Korean War, when American and South Korean forces were enveloped by the North Koreans and were in danger of being driven into the sea, MacArthur devised his boldest-ever strategy. This involved a high-risk landing behind the advancing enemy at Inchon, Korea. Most experts believed the maneuver would be impossible to carry out due to sea currents and a rough coast. When word reached him that the landing was an unmitigated success and the enemy was in full retreat, MacArthur excused himself from the group with whom he was meeting, walked a few paces away, and vomited (Manchester, 1978). At no time prior to victory had the general displayed the slightest doubt.

Finally, a willingness to work hard and a demonstrated sense of loyalty will get one noticed in most organizations. In addition, expressing a willingness to take on new responsibilities distinguishes one from the crowd. Leaders are those whom others follow. To lead one must put oneself out front.

Notes

[1] The ranks of the federal service begin at GS 1 and go GS 18. The rank of GS 15 therefore is roughly equivalent to the rank of colonel in the military.

[2] Murphy is an apocryphal foot soldier credited with a list of rules and axioms, the most famous of which is titled Murphy's Law: "If it can go wrong, it will."

References

Allison, Graham T., & Zelikow, Philip. (1999). *Essence of decision: Explaining the Cuban missile crisis.* (2nd ed.). Upper Saddle River, NJ: Longman.

American Institute of Certified Public Accountants. (2008/2009). *Code of professional conduct: Section 51, preamble.* Retrieved from www.aicpa.org/about/code/et_50.html

American Society for Public Administration. (2006). *Code of ethics.* Retrieved from http://www.aspanet.org/scriptcontent/index

Aristotle. (1998). *A Nicomachean ethics* (William David Ross, Trans.; J. L. Ackrill and J. O. Urmson, Eds.). Oxford, England: Oxford University Press.

Asprey, Robert B. (2001). *The reign of Napoleon Bonaparte.* New York: Basic Books.

Barnard, Chester I. (1968). *The functions of the executive* (30th anniv. ed.). Introduction by Kenneth R. Andrews. Cambridge, MA: Harvard University Press.

Barrett, Richard. (2006). *Building a values-driven organization: A whole systems approach to cultural transformation.* Burlington, MA: Butterworth-Heineman.

Ben-Gurion, David. (1963). *Israel: Years of challenge.* New York: Holt, Rinehart and Winston.

Bennis, Warren G. (2003). *On becoming a leader: The leadership classic.* New York: Basic Books.

Berger, Roger W. (1986). *Quality circles: Selected readings.* Quality and reliability series, vol. 9. New York: Marcel Dekker.

Burns, James MacGregor. (1978). *Leadership.* New York: Harper & Row.

Burns, James MacGregor. (2006). *Roosevelt: The soldier of freedom (1940–1945).* New York: History Book Club.

Burton, Steven J. (1980). Breach of contract and the common law duty to perform in good faith. *94 Harvard Law Review,* 369, 371.

Carman, Harry J., & Luthin, Reinhard H. (1943). *Lincoln and the patronage.* New York: Columbia University Press.

Chamberlin, Frederick. (1923). *The sayings of Queen Elizabeth.* New York: Dodd Mead.

Chernow, Ron. (2004). *Alexander Hamilton.* New York: Penguin Books.

Collins, Larry, & LaPierre, Dominique. (1997). *Freedom at midnight: The epic drama of India's struggle for independence.* New Delhi: Vikas.

Confucius. (1979). *The analects* (D. C. Lau, Trans.). New York: Penguin Books.

Connell, Evan S. (1984). *Son of the morning star.* San Francisco: North Point Press.

Cummins Engine Company. (n.d.). *Cummins Practice: Subject ethical standards.* Retrieved November 2008 from http://ethics.iit.edu/codes/coe/cummins.engine.co.ethical.standards.html

De Pree, Max. (1989). *Leadership is an art.* New York: Dell Publishing.

Deming, W. Edwards. (2000). *Out of the crisis* (2nd ed.). Cambridge, MA: MIT University Press.

Dewey, John. (1891). *Outlines of a critical theory of ethics.* Ann Arbor, MI: Register Publishing Company.

Dewey, John. (1949). *The wit and wisdom of John Dewey* (A. H. Johnson, Ed.). Boston: Beacon Press.

Douglas, Christina. (1997). *Formal mentoring programs in organizations.* Greensboro, NC: Center for Creative Leadership.

Downs, Anthony. (1957). *An economic theory of democracy.* New York: Harper.

Drucker, Peter F. (1969). *The age of discontinuity.* New York: Harper and Row.

Drucker, Peter F. (1998). Management's new paradigms. *Forbes Magazine,* October 5: 152–177.

Eisenhower, Dwight D. (1963). *Mandate for change, 1953–1956: The White House years.* Garden City, NJ: Doubleday.

Eisenhower, Dwight D. (1967). *At ease: Stories I tell to friends.* Garden City, NJ: Doubleday.

Eisenhower, Dwight D. (1998). *Eisenhower: The prewar diaries and selected papers, 1905–1941* (Daniel D. Holt, Ed.). Baltimore: Johns Hopkins University Press.

Etzioni, Amitai. (1967). Mixed scanning: A third approach to decision making. *Public Administration Review,* December: 385–92.

Fayol, Henri. (1949). *General and industrial management.* London: Pitman.

Foote, Shelby. (1974). *The Civil War: A narrative.* New York: Vintage.

Funakoshi, Gichin. (1997). *Karate-do, my way of life.* Cambridge, England: Cambridge University Press.

Gillespie, Richard. (1991). *Manufacturing knowledge: A history of the Hawthorne experiments.* Cambridge, England: Cambridge University Press.

Golding, William. (1962). *Lord of the flies.* New York: Coward-McCann.

Goleman, Daniel. (2006). *Emotional intelligence: Why it can matter more than IQ.* (10th anniv. ed.) New York: Bantam Books.

Goodwin, Doris Kearns. (1994). *No ordinary time: Franklin and Eleanor Roosevelt: The home front in World War II.* New York: Simon & Schuster.

Greenspan, Alan. (2008, October 23). Greenspan concedes error on regulation. *The New York Times.* Retrieved from http://www.nytimes.com/2008/10/24/business/economy/24panel.html

Herzberg, Frederick, Mausner, Bernard, & Bloch Snyderman, Barbara. (1993). *The motivation to work.* Edison, NJ: Transaction.

Hoffman, Jon T. (2001). *Chesty: The story of lieutenant general Lewis B. Puller, USMC.* New York: Random House.

Hoge, Warren. (1998, October 17). 2 Ulster peacemakers win the Nobel Prize. *New York Times.* Retrieved from http://query.nytimes.com/gst/fullpage.html

Holmes, Richard. (2003). *Wellington: The iron duke.* New York: HarperCollins.

Homer. (1906). *The odyssey of Homer, done into English prose.* (Samuel H. Butcher and Andrew Lang, Eds.). New York: The Macmillan Company.

http://www.elizabethi.org/us/quotes

http://www.brainyquote.com/quotes/authors/g/golda_meir.html

http://www.quotationspage.com/quotes/Indira_Gandhi

Isaacson, Walter. (2003). *Benjamin Franklin: An American life.* New York: Simon & Schuster.

Landau, Elaine. (2006). *Napoleon Bonaparte.* Minneapolis: Twenty-First Century Books.

Lawrence, T. E. (1991). *Seven pillars of wisdom.* New York: Anchor Books. Original copyright 1926, Doubleday.

Los Angeles Times. (1998, June 3). Key developments in Orange County's financial crisis: 1994 to 1998. Retrieved from http://articles.latimes.com/1998/jun/03/news/mn-56196

Machiavelli, Niccolo. (1992). *The prince* (W. K. Marriott, Trans.). New York: Alfred A. Knopf.

Manchester, William. (1978). *American Caesar: Douglas MacArthur, 1880–1964.* New York: Back Bay Books.

Marquis de Pombal. (1966). Pombal's advice on how to best govern Brazil. In E. Bradford Burns (Ed.), *A documentary history of Brazil* (pp. 132–36). New York: Alfred A Knopf.

Maslow, Abraham H. (1987). *Motivation and personality.* New York: HarperCollins.

Mayo, Elton. (2003). *The human problems of an industrial civilization: The early sociology of management and organizations.* London: Routledge.

McCain, John. (1999). *Faith of my fathers.* With Mark Salter. New York: Random House.

McClelland, David. (1988). *Human motivation.* Cambridge, England: Cambridge University Press.

McGregor, Douglas. (2005). *The human side of enterprise.* (Annot. ed.). New York: McGraw Hill.

McLuhan, Marshall. (1962). *The Gutenberg galaxy: The making of typographical man.* Toronto: University of Toronto Press.

Meacham, Jon. (2003). *Franklin and Winston: An intimate portrait of an epic friendship.* New York: Random House.

Meacham, Jon. (2008). *American lion: Andrew Jackson in the White House.* New York: Random House.

Miles, Raymond E. (1975). *Theories of management: Implications for organizational behavior and development.* New York: McGraw-Hill.

Morris, Aldon D. (1984). *The origins of the civil rights movement: Black communities organizing for political change.* New York: Free Press.

Neustadt, Richard E. (1991). *Presidential power and the modern presidents: The politics of leadership.* New York: The Free Press.

Nietzsche, Friedrich. (2000). *Basic writings of Nietzsche* (W. Kaufmann, Ed. and Trans.). New York: The Modern Library.

Oppenheim, David, & Goldsmith, Douglas F. (Eds.). (2007). *Attachment theory in clinical work with children: Bridging the gap between research and practice.* New York: Guilford Press.

Osborne, David, & Gaebler, Ted. (1993). *Reinventing government: How the entrepreneurial spirit is transforming the public sector.* New York: Plume.

Plato. (1901). *The republic* (Henry Davis, Trans.). New York: Walter Dunne.

Porter, Lyman W., & Bigley, Gregory A. (Eds.). (1995). *Human relations: Theory and developments.* Ashgate: Dartmouth.

Porter, Lyman W., Lawler, Edward E. III, & Hackman, J. Richard. (1975). *Behavior in organizations.* New York: McGraw Hill.

Porter, Michael E. (1998). *Competitive strategy: Techniques for analyzing industries and competitors.* New York: Free Press.

PricewaterhouseCoopers. (2006). *The crisis in federal government succession planning: What is being done about it.* Retrieved from http://www.pwc.com/ Extweb/pwcpublications.nsf/docid/45C77C53C31B97D0852571C4007229D8/ $File/wfp-succession-planning-final-a.pdf

Ramonet, Ignacio. (2006). *Fidel Castro: Biografía a dos voces.* Barcelona: Debate.

Reeves, C. D. (1988). *Philosopher kings: The arguments of Plato's Republic.* Princeton, NJ: Princeton University Press.

Richelieu, Armand Jean du Plessis. (1961). *The political testament of Cardinal Richelieu* (Henry Bertram Hill, Trans.). Madison: University of Wisconsin Press.

Ross, William David. (1998). Introduction. In *A Nicomachean ethics* by Aristotle (William David Ross, Trans.; J. L. Ackrill and J. O. Urmson, Eds.). Oxford, England: Oxford University Press.

Runyon, Damon. (1952). *Runyon on Broadway.* (Omnibus ed.). London: Constable.

Sarbanes-Oxley Act of 2002. Public Law 107-204, 116 Statute 745, July 30, 2002.

Schlesinger, Arthur. (1965). *A thousand days: John F. Kennedy in the White House.* New York: Houghton Mifflin.

Schmidt, Michael. (2008, November 25). Eleven months later some praise for baseball. *New York Times.* Retrieved from http://www.nytimes.com/2008/ 11/26/sports/baseball/26mitchell.html

Shirer, William L. (1959). *The rise and fall of the Third Reich.* New York: Simon & Schuster.

Simon, Herbert A. (1984). *Models of bounded rationality: Vol. 1, economic analysis and public policy.* Cambridge, MA: MIT Press.

Sperlich, Peter W. (1969). Bargaining and overload: An essay on presidential power. In Aaron Wildavsky (Ed.), *The presidency* (pp. 168–92). Boston: Little Brown.

Steers, Richard M., & Porter, Lyman W. (1983). *Motivation and work behavior.* (3rd ed.). New York: McGraw Hill.

Stogdill, Ralph M. (Ed.). (1957). *Leader behavior: Its description and measurement.* Columbus: Bureau of Business Research, Ohio State University.

Sun Tzu. (1988). *The art of war* (James Clavell, Ed.). New York: Delta Books.

Sutton, Kurt M. (1998). Chesty Puller: Everyone needs a hero. *Marine Magazine,* August.

Sylvia, Ronald D. (1995). Presidential decision making and civil rights. *Presidential Studies Quarterly, 25*(3), 391–411.

Sylvia, Ronald D., & Meyer, C. Kenneth. (2001). *Public personnel administration* (2nd ed.). Fort Worth, TX: Harcourt.

Sylvia, Ronald D., & Sylvia, Kathleen M. (2004). *Program planning and evaluation for public managers.* Long Grove, IL: Waveland Press.

Taibo, Paco Ignacio II. (1996). *Ernesto Guevara, también conocido como el Che.* Mexico City: Planeta.

Taibo, Paco Ignacio, II. (2006). *Pancho Villa: Una biografía narrativa.* Mexico City: Planeta.

Thompson, James D. (2003). *Organizations in action: Social science bases of administrative theory.* Edison, NJ: Transaction Publishers.

Townsend, Robert C. (2007). *Up the organization: How to stop the corporation from stifling people and strangling profits.* San Francisco: Jossey Bass.

Tracy, Nicholas. (1996). *Nelson's battles: The art of victory in the age of sail.* Annapolis, MD: Naval Institute Press.

Truman, Harry S. (1948). *Executive order 9981: Establishing the President's Committee on Equality of Treatment and Opportunity in the Armed Services,* July 26, 1948. Retrieved from http://www.ourdocuments.gov/doc.php?flash=true&doc=84.

Truman, Harry S. (1955). *Memoirs of Harry S. Truman: Years of trial and hope.* New York: Doubleday.

U.S. Supreme Court. (1954). *Brown v. Board of Education of Topeka Kansas,* 347 U.S. 483 (1954).

Vroom, Victor. (1964). *Work and motivation.* (3rd ed.). New York: John Wiley and Sons.

Walt Disney (Producer). (1951). *Alice in Wonderland* [Motion picture]. United States: Walt Disney Animation Studio.

War Library. (1988). *Tet Offensive, 1968: Turning point in the Vietnam War.* Retrieved from http://members.aol.com/veterans/warlib65.htm

Weber, Max. (1946). *Essays in sociology* (H. H. Gerth & C. Wright Mills, Eds. and Trans.). Oxford, England: Oxford University Press.

Weber, Max. (1957). *The theory of social and economic organization* (Talcott Parsons, Ed.). Glencoe, IL: Free Press.

Westbrook, John. (1991). *John Dewey and American democracy.* Ithaca, NY: Cornell University Press.

Wilson, Woodrow. (1898). *The state: Elements of historical and practical politics.* Boston: D. C. Heath.

Wolff, Tobias. (1994). *In pharaoh's army: Memories of the lost war.* New York: Random House.

Index